Secret Growing With Substance

Working with Children and Young People Affected by Familial Substance Misuse

Edited by

Fiona Harbin

and

Michael Murphy

First published in 2006 by:
Russell House Publishing Ltd.
4 St. George's House
Uplyme Road
Lyme Regis
Dorset DT7 3LS
Tel: 01297-443948
Fax: 01297-442722
e-mail: help@russellhouse.co.uk
www.russellhouse.co.uk

British Library Cataloguing-in-publication Data:
A catalogue record for this book is available from the British Library.

ISBN: 1-903855-66-7; 978-1-903855-66-9

Typeset by TW Typesetting, Plymouth, Devon
Printed by ???

About Russell House Publishing

Russell House Publishing aims to publish innovative and valuable materials
to help managers, practitioners, trainers, educators and students.

Our full catalogue covers: social policy, working with young people,
helping children and families, care of older people, social care, combating
social exclusion, revitalising communities and working with offenders.

Full details can be found at www.russellhouse.co.uk and we are pleased to
send out information to you by post. Our contact details are on this page.

We are always keen to receive feedback on publications and new ideas
for future projects.

Contents

Preface   vi

Acknowledgements   vii

About the Authors   viii

Chapter 1   What do we Know About Children and Young People
            who Grow up in Substance Misusing Households?   1
            Michael Murphy and Fiona Harbin

Chapter 2   Reaching Out: Promoting Resilience in the Children
            of Substance Misusers   12
            Richard Velleman and Lorna Templeton

Chapter 3   Using Group Work to Support Young People Living
            with Substance Misuse   28
            Ellen Wheeler

Chapter 4   Separation, Substance Misuse and Children in
            Alternative Care   42
            Deborah Evans and Fiona Harbin

Chapter 5   Children, Alcohol and Family Violence   55
            Deborah Evans

Chapter 6   The Roller Coaster of Change: The Process of
            Parental Change from a Child's Perspective   80
            Fiona Harbin

Chapter 7   Developing Whole Family Treatment Services   95
            Fiona Harbin and Michael Murphy

Chapter 8   Where it all Begins: Growing Up and the Helping
            Relationship   110
            Phil Harris

Chapter 9   The Impact of Sibling Substance Misuse on Children
            and Young People   126
            Nicola Taylor and Jackie Kearney

Chapter 10   **Setting up a Substance Misuse Project for Young People**   **138**
Tom O'Loughlin and Dave Seaber

For Carly and Dylan

Preface

Secret Lives is the sister volume to *Substance Misuse and Child Care* (RHP, 2000). It is a book that offers new and challenging insights into the task of working with children and young people who are affected by substance misuse. This includes the needs of children brought up in substance misusing households, and young people who are beginning to misuse substances themselves.

Because these children and young people have contact with a multiplicity of practice groups, we have invited practitioners, managers and researchers from several different backgrounds to contribute to this work.

Some readers may be curious about our choice of title. This name comes from a nine year old who suggested a name for their children's group: *Secret Lives, because we can talk about what is really going on at home.*

Acknowledgements

We would like to acknowledge the tremendous support offered by Bolton Substance Misuse Research Group and also the encouragement of Bolton ACPC/LHSCB and Bolton DAAT.

About the Authors

Deborah Evans is a Team Manager in Bolton based in an assessment and therapy team. She has worked in various settings in social care for 30 years, primarily in child protection, with a special interest in the effects of domestic violence on the lives of children and young people. Deborah has led on developing group work for children exposed to domestic violence and for women living with partners who pose a risk to their children.

Fiona Harbin is the Multi Agency Substance Misuse Training Coordinator for Bolton. She qualified as a social worker in 1989. Going on to work in children and families teams in Wigan and Bolton, she moved to Bolton's Child Protection Unit in 1996, where she worked specifically with children and families where substance misuse was affecting parenting.

Over the last few years Fiona has been involved in the development of specialised services in Bolton for substance misusing families. She has helped develop practice guidance for multi-agency staff, has co-edited with Michael Murphy *Substance Misuse and Child Care* (2001), and contributed a chapter with Michael Murphy to *Assessment in Childcare*, edited by Calder and Hackett (2003). Fiona has a particular interest in the impact of substance misuse on young people and contributed to the recent research publication *The Highs and Lows of Family Life; Familial Substance Misuse from a Child's Perspective* (Kearney et al., 2005).

Phil Harris has worked in the drug misuse field for the last 14 years as a practitioner, manager and supervisor. In the 1990s he helped establish drug services for young people in Bristol and the adult counselling models he developed are used as a national blueprint of good practice. Now a freelance trainer, writer and consultant, he has worked on a diverse range of treatment programmes across the UK, Sweden, Holland and Dubai. He was also an advisor for the WHO in Macedonia. A visiting lecturer and advisor to the School of Policy Studies at Bristol University and the US BICEP programme, he has published over 20 articles on treatment and effectiveness. His first book, *Drug Induced* (Russell House Publishing) was published in 2005, and his second *Empathy for the Devil* (Russell House Publishing) is due for release in 2006.

Jackie Kearney has been active in researching and teaching in the area of substance misuse for several years. As a research fellow, a research manager and a research consultant Jackie has managed and contributed to several qualitative and quantitative studies concerning drug use and service needs, utilising multiple indicators including privileged access fieldwork, pilot studies with children and young people and secondary data sources. She has also been a senior lecturer on an applied community studies programme.

Michael Murphy is currently a senior lecturer at Salford University, where he teaches on the post-qualifying child care award. Michael trained as a social worker and a counsellor and has been involved in child care for 30 years. Michael's research interests include interagency collaboration in childcare, partnership working, substance misuse and family life and stress in social care. Michael has published widely in all four areas.

Tom O'Loughlin is Head of Service for Children's Resources with Bolton Children's Services. He is a qualified social worker with a history of working in all sections of children and family services including child protection, assessments and support for looked after children. He was actively involved in the development of Bolton's Child Concern model (a multi-agency system for all children in need). He has a strong interest in and commitment to developing substance misuse services for young people, children and families.

Dave Seaber has worked as a child care practitioner with social services departments and with the NSPCC. For the last three years he has managed the 360° project – Bolton's Children and Young People's Substance Misuse Service.

Nik Taylor completed her undergraduate studies and her doctorate in sociology at Manchester Metropolitan University in the UK. She then went on to teach sociology and to research a number of different projects at the Universities of Edinburgh and Salford. She recently joined Central Queensland University from the University of Oxford where she was working on a number of projects addressing gender and health. Her areas of interest are the sociology of human-animal relationships, particularly links between domestic violence, child abuse and companion animal harm, and families and parenting, in particular drug using parents and their children. Dr Taylor is a member of the Research Advisory Board of Queensland Centre for Domestic and Family Violence Research and the Board of the Centre for Animal Liberation Affairs.

Lorna Templeton has a degree in Sociology and a Masters in Social Research, and has previously worked at addiction centres in London and Toronto. Lorna has worked at the Mental Health Research and Development Unit since 1997, where she is Senior Researcher and Deputy Manager. Her main area of research is around the impact of alcohol and drug problems on the family, and developing and evaluating clinically appropriate interventions and services for these family members. Lorna is also the Manager of this research programme within the R&D Unit. Lorna is also a former Chair of the New Directions in the Study of Alcohol Group, a member of Alcohol Concern's Children and Families Forum and a member of the Encare network, an EU-wide collaboration to develop resources for professionals who come into contact or work with children living in families where there are parental alcohol problems. She has published several peer-reviewed publications, co-authored several book chapters and presented widely at conferences and seminars.

Richard Velleman BSc, MSc, PhD, FBPsS, FRSS, C. Psychol. is a clinical psychologist, Professor of Mental Health Research at the University of Bath, and director of the joint Avon and Wiltshire Mental Health Partnership NHS Trust (AWP)/University of Bath: Mental Health Research and Development Unit. He has a keen interest in evidence-based service development, and has founded statutory addictions services, helped develop the Families and Psychosis service within AWP, worked as an NHS Trust Board Director, undertaken many externally funded research projects and published very widely on a range of mental health topics, especially related to the impact of addiction on families.

Ellen Wheeler is a qualified social worker working at 360°, Bolton's Young People's Substance Misuse Service, and is one of the longest standing members of the team, joining the service in 2000. Prior to this she had many years of experience working within the family support services. Ellen has been pivotal in setting up and facilitating groups for young people living with sibling and parental substance misuse. She has developed group work programmes specifically to meet the needs of these young people, taking into account their holistic needs.

Ellen played a major role in the undertaking of the recently published research *The Highs and Lows of Family Life: Familial Substance Misuse from a Child's Perspective* (Kearney et al., 2005) and continues to have a particular interest in the effects of substance misuse on families.

Chapter 1

What do we Know About Children and Young People who Grow up in Substance Misusing Households?

Michael Murphy and Fiona Harbin

Introduction

This book is not about substance misuse per se. It is about working with children around the impact of substance misuse on their lives. It is also about working with young people who begin to choose to use substances.

Children are independent actors in their own lives, with rights, perspectives and cultures: 'it is now recognised that children and young people have a unique cultural perspective and therefore may differ from adults in their views and experiences about matters that affect them' (Kearney, 2001: 3–4). This book attempts to discover some of these different views and experiences and offers them back to adult practitioners to better pursue their work with children and young people.

We live in a society that finds it convenient to presume that substance misuse is a user, adult-only issue, or a matter for crime prevention. Because of this a great deal of the literature on substance misuse is about adults and their needs. But we know that a large percentage of adults who misuse substances are parents. Parental use impacts significantly on children (ACMD, 2003) and substance use of older children can impact significantly on their families (Barnard, 2005). This book is concerned with the needs of these children and young people and the needs and understanding of the people who work with them.

This is not the last book on this subject area that you may need to read. It does not claim to bequeath an omniscient knowledge. We are aware that the more research that is done in this area the more complex the messages become. But what it does offer are specific and often original insights into children's work and children's worlds.

This book begins from the premise that, although there are significant differences between misuse of alcohol and illicit drugs (Harwin and Forrester, 2005) some of which are discussed later in the book, the similarities of their effect upon children and families mean that it is important to consider them together. This is why the generic term substance is used throughout the book to encompass alcohol, illicit street drugs and misused prescribed medication.

The incidence and significance of substance misuse

'Parental problem drug use can and does cause serious harm to children at every age from conception to adulthood'. This is one of six key messages from *Hidden Harm*, the report of an inquiry by the Advisory Council on the Misuse of Drugs (ACMD, 2003). This document revealed, perhaps for the first time, the true extent of the impact of parental problematic drug use in the United Kingdom. The report estimated that there are between 250,000 and 350,000 children of problem drug users in the UK. This figure represents about 2 to 3 per cent of under 16 year olds in England and Wales and 4 to 6 per cent in Scotland. If we were to include alcohol dependence (Bancroft et al., 2004) this figure dramatically increases by over 900,000. The substance misuse of at least one parent significantly impacts on well over a million children and young people, one in ten of Britain's child population.

Although the scale of the problem has been revealed, these figures are unlikely to surprise those working with children. Over the last two decades child care practitioners have seen a dramatic increase in the impact of parental substance misuse on the children and young people they are working with (Harbin and Murphy, 2000; Mahoney and MacKechnie, 2001). Parental substance misuse is a significant factor for children on the child protection register (Dore et al., 1995; Forester, 2000; Harwin and Forrester, 2005), for children in the looked after system (Harwin and Forrester, 2005), for children and young people involved in the criminal justice system; for those involved with child and adolescent mental health services and for those seeking help from young people's substance misuse services.

At all levels of child care, practitioners are working with children who have experienced their parent's substance misuse. A proportion of these children will go on to significantly use substance themselves, but a large proportion will not.

At no point do we suggest that all parents who misuse substances are inadequate: 'It should be recognised by agencies dealing with drug using parents that the children are not at risk of abuse solely by virtue of the fact that the parent is a drug user' (SCODA, 1997: 2). But it is likely that many of their dependant children may, at best, be in need of some extra support to negotiate the tricky path through adolescence to their own adulthood and parenthood.

Our child care system (Bolton ACPC, 2001) defines abuse of a child as 'inflicting harm, or by failing to act to prevent harm. Children may be abused in a family or in an institution or community setting; by those known to them or, more rarely, by a stranger'. This encompasses a wide variety of risks to children. When considering those living with parental substance misuse, it is important to ensure that we consider those potential risks posed by external factors as well as those present in the home environment (Barnard, 2002).

The levels of risk and the nature of these risks are difficult to specifically categorise, as they can vary greatly. Those children and young people who are most vulnerable are often not only living with parental substance misuse, but may also experience domestic violence, poverty, social exclusion, school exclusion, parenting problems, lack of family support, parental mental and physical health problems and exposure to violence and offending behaviour (Alison, 2000; Cleaver et al., 1999; Mahoney and MacKechnie, 2001; Bancroft et al., 2004, Kearney et al., 2005; Harwin and Forrester, 2005). Some of these factors can relate specifically to the impact of substance misuse, but for many families their existing problems are exacerbated by the use of substances. Often substance misuse is a way of coping with the multitude of problems stemming from social deprivation and exclusion (Gilman, 2000). For these reasons substance misuse cannot be seen in isolation but must be seen as part of a whole picture. 'It is important not to generalise, or make assumptions about the impact on a child of parental drug and alcohol misuse, it is however important that the implications for the child are properly assessed' (DoH, 1999: 9).

The child's view

Whilst parents and practitioners (Kearney and Taylor, 2001) recognise some of the difficulties for children living in substance dependent households, children and young people themselves often express different concerns. There are recurring themes which paint a picture of their own, child-centred reality. A research project that worked with children in our area (Kearney et al., 2005) identified the following concerns that children themselves express:

- *Born withdrawing from a substance*
  The impact of severe substance dependence makes its first appearance in the womb, with variable impact on the health and well being of the child (Macrory and Harbin, 2000). At birth the child of a substance dependant mother will frequently experience a very shaky start with withdrawal symptoms that can extend for several weeks. In terms of Hackett's (2003) 'relational fit' between parent and child, a new vulnerable parent can be faced with a baby who is very hard to care for and soothe.
- *Lack of attachment to parental figures/repetitive experiences of separation and loss*
  Children in substance misusing households frequently experience separation and loss in the form of unpredictable parental absence. This can be due to death, arrest and incarceration, hospitalisation, severe family disputes leading to separation: 'sometimes you might get money, sometimes you might get arrested. Anything can happen' (Mahoney and MacKechnie, 2001: 16). For the child the repetitive experience of being 'let down' can be significant: one child told the researcher that 'you get used to it after a while'. (However, witnessing the children's frustration and sadness when their parent failed to turn up, it certainly didn't appear that they had

got used to it, Kearney et al., 2005: 20). All these experiences can significantly impact on the child's attachment and sense of self-esteem.

- *Poverty and lack of provision of basic needs*
  A minority of substance dependent families will not experience significant poverty. This is usually due to their ability to generate money, frequently on an illegal basis (Kearney et al., 2005). The majority of families however, often surviving on benefit, will find it hard to meet the cost of substance dependence and the basic cost of child care: 'It's just like, sometimes we have no food, which really upsets me' (Kearney et al., 2005: 20).

- *Age inappropriate levels of responsibility of young carers*
  Most children interviewed talk about the concern they have for their parent's well being. There are a multitude of ways that use of a substance can exhibit itself on the immediate health and well being of the parent. Parents may experience lethargy and sleep, mental health problems such as paranoia, anxiety or depression, physical health problems, irritability, lack of co-ordination, forgetfulness, incoherent speech, drunkenness, and, in the worse cases, loss of consciousness or death. Not only do many of these factors impact on parenting capacity but also a child or young person in the household may have to deal with much of the physical and emotional care for their parent and younger siblings: 'Rebecca doesn't go to school. She stays at home to look after Julie and Christopher (the younger children). She cleans up in the house. She has to mind them' (CW, in Mahoney and MacKechnie, 2001: 17). Kearney et al. (2005) noted the frequency with which older children, particularly girls, would take inappropriate responsibility for their siblings: 'I get sick of looking after (younger siblings) 'cos they just need help all of the time and it's really hard work. I just wish they could look after themselves a bit more' (15). Holding an adult's responsibility for child care, without an adult's knowledge, experience and power can be difficult. Some children will deny that it is a problem for them: 'I do a lot of work in the house now, more than I used to, but it's my choice to do it. I like to cook for everyone and help out. I know I do more than most young teens do but I want to do it' (Kearney et al., 2005: 15).

- *Unpredictable, inconsistent lifestyle and instability*
  Children and parents identify the destructive effect of broken promises (Kearney and Taylor, 2001; Kearney et al., 2005). This could be as simple as a parent not getting fish fingers for tea or as upsetting as a mother who forgets her child's birthday. Children had reported that they had grown not to trust their parents, as nothing they said was carried through. Not only did this affect the attachment and relationship between parents and children but also impacted on the young people's negative expectations of other adults.

- *Stigma and shame*
  One message that our children have given very clearly to us is that they feel the stigma and shame of substance misuse very strongly: 'Some of my friends at school, they heard about it, and then it was like Drugs! Drugs! Your parents are taking

drugs and all that' (Kearney et al., 2005: 17). Barnard (1995) states that this shame and stigma was also felt when the user was a sibling: 'Having a brother or a sister with a drug problem was both shaming and embarrassing. It was embarrassing to see them in public under the influence of drugs or begging in the streets' (23). In their community life, the children of drug using parents can be put down, belittled and bullied because society's attitudes towards substance dependence exacerbates negative community attitudes. This stigma further isolates children, and adds no value to their lives.

- *Living with secrecy and isolation*
This type of secrecy is partly the result of the fear and shame of substance dependence, leading to children keeping secret what is happening in their family and being reluctant to invite friends to their home. It is also an internal sort of secrecy where parents, in their attempt to shield the child from their dependence, will never allow the child to talk openly about it: 'I knew something was wrong but then dad talked to me about it. I wanted them to be open and honest rather than try to hide it from me. That helped' (Kearney et al., 2005: 14).

    If children can't talk outside or inside the family, they have no way of resolving their distress and fear.

- *Lifelines*
On the other hand, children also report particularly helpful responses from people that Doyle (1997) describes as lifelines: 'the most important single survival factor was that each had at least one person who gave them unconditional positive regard; someone who thought well of them and made them feel important' (338). In our study this included grandparents, siblings, other relatives and professionals like teachers. These lifelines and the resilience they promote are discussed further in Chapter 2.

- *Sibling substance misuse*
Children themselves have also identified the significance of sibling substance misuse (Wheeler, Ch. 3). The majority of parents using substances will try to ensure that their children are not exposed to this, with varying degrees of success. However, that intention to protect children from substances is not as apparent when the user is an older sibling (Kearney et al., 2005). Anecdotally, it would appear that a significant minority of children are introduced to substances by an older sibling, an issue which is often not included in our assessments of risk. The importance of siblings is discussed further in Chapter 9.

- *Exposure to violence and offending*
There are recognised and well documented links between domestic violence, physical abuse and alcohol dependency (Velleman and Orford, 1999; Harwin and Forrester, 2005) and an accepted view that high alcohol consumption can lead to violence inside and outside the home (see Chapter 5). The evidence for linking illicit drug misuse with domestic violence is less clearly defined. Kearney and Taylor (2001) found that parents reported that children were often exposed to high levels of family conflict as a result of drug misuse. The high levels of tension and pressure

within a home over finances and maintaining a dependency on a drug could escalate to abusive arguments and violence between parents, which were often witnessed by the children.

The culture of violence and threats which underpins the world of illicit drugs can also impinge on family life. Use of weapons and firearms appears to be increasing in the conflicts for control of the drug market, and the potential for harm to children in these situations cannot be underestimated. There are well-reported tragic cases of children having been shot and killed in circumstances relating to their parents drug misuse.

Although these may be extreme examples, studies indicate that many children living with substance misuse are also living in the constant shadow of violence and threats to their family. For many children this violent experience can become normalised: 'Some children described violent events in a matter of fact manner, expressing no shock, fear or understanding of the danger of the circumstances' (Kearney et al., 2005: 19). Abuse from neighbours, vandalism to their homes and threats from dealers becomes a normal part of the everyday lives for a significant minority of children (Kearney et al., 2005; Wheeler, 2005; Harwin and Forrester, 2005). This acceptance of extreme levels of threats and violence shows itself in children talking in a matter of fact way about stabbings and beatings within their homes or in the community.

Surrounded by high levels of violence, some young people not only accept it as normal but have also come to expect it. This begins to affect the way they interpret life, their own behaviour, and their ability to assess risky situations for themselves. In certain circumstances young people may place themselves in extremely dangerous situations and perceive this as safe (Kearney et al., 2005). This will inevitably make them more vulnerable to potential risks outside the home. This may be exacerbated if their parents own problems limit their ability to predict dangers for their children and inhibit their ability to know their children's whereabouts if they are late arriving home or are absent for long periods.

This adds a further dimension to the work done to ensure the safety of children. Whilst practitioners are becoming skilled in assessment and interventions with parents and children, the unquantifiable risks posed by individuals from outside the home are far more complex and can lead to professional dilemmas in decision making.

Practice Scenario 1

Julie, a young mother, dependent on heroin and crack, with two young children, was managing to parent reasonably well, with family support. Julie then received threats to her life which the police said should be taken seriously. The professionals involved were confused. The risk to the children was real, but was not coming from inside the family.

We enter a field of probabilities and risk measurement but the risks are immediate and potentially life threatening. One very young child in our area was killed in a substance related incident whilst accompanying their carer to the shop to buy sweets. The risks to the children in these circumstances can be exacerbated by the feeling of helplessness of the workers and their genuine concerns about safety for themselves, whilst wanting to ensure the safety of the children.

● *The difficult issue of treatment*
 Treatment and change around substance misuse is always difficult. But as adult practitioners or users, we always see treatment as a positive way forward. For children the issue of treatment is much more complicated than this. For some children and young people the instability of substance use is more manageable than their parents engaging with treatment and then repeatedly relapsing. They understand the home situation and make sense of it in early childhood. This internal working model is often upset by parental change leading to distress, confusion and self-blame (see Chapter 6).

This list is not exhaustive, but represents some of the experiences of young people living in substance misusing households. Not only can a substance affect the immediate well being of a parent but the impact of dependency over a period of time can also detrimentally affect the lifestyle of the parents and therefore the family as a whole (Velleman and Orford, 1999).

The children in our studies, however, show strong signs of creativity and tenacity. They will actively attempt to get their own needs met and to meet the needs of their siblings. They strive to be resilient. Their young lives seem to involve a constant shuttling between the risks that are around them and the resilience that they are striving for. We will also see that this shuttle also involves the swing between the optimism that they and their family are going to be alright, and the pessimism that accompanies repetitive reverses in their lives.

Interagency and intersystem working

The final point that we would like to make at the start of this book is about collaboration. Many authors (Forrester, 2000; Murphy and Oulds, 2000; ACDM, 2003; Bancroft et al., 2004 and Harwin and Forrester, 2005) have emphasised the special hurdles to collaboration that familial substance misuse presents. Superimposed on the usual issues that concern the collaboration of staff from child care agencies (Calder, 2003; Murphy, 2004) are the particular issues that concern the collaboration of staff from adult-oriented substance systems (Murphy and Oulds, 2000; Kearney et al., 2000 and Harwin and Forrester, 2005). It is certainly the case that all the interagency changes in child care emanating from the green paper *Every Child Matters* will have a very limited impact in this area. Furthermore, the government response to *Hidden Harm* (DfES, 2005) indicates no new initiatives in this collaborative area.

Over the last five years there has been a much-needed increase in research studies and publications on the impact of parental substance misuse. As our knowledge increases and we become more aware of the impact of parental substance misuse on all aspects of children's lives we are better able to assess and identify the risks and potential risks for children and young people. However, it can leave us with more questions about how we can address the issues and what are the most appropriate ways forward to ensure the safety of young people.

What is certain is that the drastic 'solutions' of care or residential provision will only be suitable or appropriate for a very small number of children. For the vast majority it is the assistance that is given directly to them, their parents and their extended families that will make a significant difference to their lives.

By ensuring we undertake thorough assessments of children and their families using the *Framework for Assessment of Children in Need and their Families* (DoH, 2000) as a guide and ensuring we incorporate more relevant questions on substances (Harbin and Murphy, 2003), we can begin to create a clearer picture of each individual child, parent and family and we can begin to discover their individual need. This book does not claim to make working with children affected by substance easy. This task is complex, multi-faceted and full of pitfalls. What it does do however, is to provide a platform for its contributors to share their knowledge and expertise more widely. This, we hope, will significantly impact on child care practice.

About this book

This book is written by a group of practitioners, managers, academics and researchers who have come together to share their experience and knowledge about working with children and young people around familial substance misuse. The book contains ten chapters.

Chapter 2 by Richard Velleman and Lorna Templeton explore what children need in substance dependent families to be resilient.

Chapter 3 by Ellen Wheeler explores the usefulness and power of group work intervention when working with children brought up in substance misusing households.

Chapter 4 by Deborah Evans and Fiona Harbin explore the needs of children brought up in substance misusing households when they arrive in alternative care.

Chapter 5 by Deborah Evans explores the impact for children of the crossover between substance misuse and domestic violence.

Chapter 6 by Fiona Harbin explores the difficult issues of treatment and change from a child's point of view.

Chapter 7 by Fiona Harbin and Michael Murphy explore the whole family approach to familial substance misuse and child care.

Chapter 8 by Phil Harris begins by examining the issues involved in developing relationships with adolescents that encourage change and resilience.

Chapter 9 by Nik Taylor and Jackie Kearney examines the impact of sibling substance misuse on other children in the family.

Chapter 10 by Tom O'Loughlin and Dave Seaber outline the setting up of a multi-disciplinary service for older children and adolescents around their substance misuse.

Two more chapters were commissioned for the book, but were not available at time of publication. Both individual subject areas are worthy of a whole publication. The first is around working with children from minority ethnic communities around familial substance misuse. We are conscious that the task of developing relationships with black and minority ethnic children around substance misuse is a highly complex one, made far more complex by the child and the community's view on substance use and the child and community's relationship with the practitioner agency. This book concerns the difficult nature of practitioners developing relationships with children around substance. There is evidence that a child's minority status can exaggerate this difficulty (Patel, 2000). The second subject area is that of substance misuse and child and adolescent mental health problems. Again the complexity of this subject area increases with each new piece of research (Barnard, 2005). For some young people, indulgence in substance use will exaggerate an existing vulnerability to mental health problems (Crome, 2004). Other young people will actively use substances to self-medicate to help with internal distress, anguish and turmoil (Sutherland, 2004).

Whether you choose to read the book as a whole, or 'dip' in to a chapter that seems particularly pertinent, we hope that the book inspires interest, is useful for practice and may even be helpful in inspiring changes in practice.

References

Advisory Committee on the Misuse of Drugs (2003) *Hidden Harm.* London: HMSO.

Alison, L. (2000) What are the Risks to Children of Parental Substance Misuse? In Harbin, F. and Murphy, M. (2000) *Substance Misuse and Child Care.* Lyme Regis: Russell House Publishing.

Bancroft, A. et al. (2004) *Parental Drug and Alcohol Misuse: Resilience and Transition among Young People.* York: Joseph Rowntree Foundation.

Barnard, M. (2002) Drugs versus Children. *zero2nineteen* (October).

Barnard, M. (2005) *Drugs in the Family.* York: Joseph Rowntree Foundation.

Bolton Area Child Protection Committee (2000) *Child Concern Handbook: Working Together to Safeguard Children.* Bolton ACPC.

Calder, M. (2003) The Assessment Framework: A Critique and Reformulation. In Calder, M. and Hackett, S. *Assessment in Child Care.* Lyme Regis: Russell House Publishing.

Cleaver, H., Unell, I. and Aldgate, J. (1999) *Children's Needs: Parenting Capacity.* London: HMSO.

Crome, I. (2004) Psychiatric Co-morbidity. In Crome, I. et al. (Eds.) *Young People and Substance Misuse.* London: Gaskell.

Department of Health (1999) *Working Together to Safeguard Children: A Guide to Interagency Working to Safeguard and Promote the Welfare of Children.* London: HMSO.

Department of Health (2000) *Framework for the Assessment of Children in Need and their Families.* London: HMSO.

Dore, M., Doris, J. and Wright, P. (1995) Identifying Substance Abuse in Maltreating Families: A Child Welfare Challenge. *Child Abuse and Neglect.* 19: 5, 531–44.

Doyle, C. (1997) Emotional Abuse of Children: Issues for Intervention. *Child Abuse Review.* 6: 330–42.

Elliot, E. et al. (1998) *Fit to be a Parent: The Needs of Drug Using Parents in Salford and Trafford.* Salford: PHRRC Research Report No. 8.

Forrester, D. (2000) Parental Substance Misuse and Child Protection in a British Sample. *Child Abuse Review.* 19: 235–46.

Gilman, M. (2000) Social Exclusion and Drug Using Parents. In Harbin, F. and Murphy, M. *Substance Misuse and Child Care.* Lyme Regis: Russell House Publishing.

Hackett, S. (2003) *A Framework for Assessing Parenting Capacity.* In Calder, M. and Hackett, S. *Assessment in Child Care.* Lyme Regis: Russell House Publishing.

Harbin, F. and Murphy, M. (Eds.) (2000) *Substance Misuse and Childcare: How to Understand, Assist, and Intervene when Drugs Affect Parenting.* Lyme Regis: Russell House Publishing.

Harbin, F. and Murphy, M. (2003) *The Assessment of Parental Substance Misuse and its Impact on Childcare.* In Calder, M. and Hackett, S. (Eds.) *Assessment in Childcare: Using and Developing Frameworks for Practice.* Lyme Regis: Russell House Publishing.

Harwin, J. and Forrester, D. (2005) *A Study of Social Work with Families in which Parents Misuse Drugs or Alcohol.* London: Nuffield Foundation.

Kearney, J. and Taylor, N. (2001) *The Highs and Lows of Family Life: Research Report.* Salford: University of Salford.

Kearney, P., Lenin, E. and Rosen, G. (2000) *Alcohol, Drug and Mental Health Problems: Working with Families.* London: NISW.

Kearney, J., Harbin, F., Murphy, M., Wheeler, E. and Whittle, J. (2005) *The Highs and Lows of Family Life: Familial Substance Misuse from a Child's Perspective.* Bolton: Bolton ACPC.

Macrory, F. and Harbin, F. (2000) *Substance Misuse and Pregnancy.* In Harbin, F. and Murphy, M. (2000) *Substance Misuse and Childcare.* Lyme Regis: Russell House Publishing.

Mahoney, C. and MacKechnie, S. (2001) *In a Different World: Parental Drug and Alcohol Use: A Consultation Into its Effects on Children and Families in Liverpool.* Liverpool: LHA.

Murphy, M. (2004) *Developing Collaborative Relationships in Interagency Child Protection Work.* Lyme Regis: Russell House Publishing.

Murphy, M. and Oulds, G. (2000) Establishing and Developing Co-operative Links between Substance Misuse and Child Protection Systems. In Harbin, F. and Murphy, M. (2000) *Substance Misuse and Childcare.* Lyme Regis: Russell House Publishing.

Orford, J. and Velleman, R. (1990) Offspring of Parents with Drinking Problems: Drinking and Drug Taking as Young Adults. *British Journal of Addictions*, 85.

Patel, K. (2000) *The Missing Drug Users: Minority Ethnic Drug Users and their Children.* In Harbin, F. and Murphy, M. *Substance Misuse and Child Care.* Lyme Regis: Russell House Publishing.

Sutherland, I. (2004) *Adolescent Substance Misuse.* Lyme Regis: Russell House Publishing.

SCODA (1997) *Drug Using Parents: Policy Guidelines for Interagency Working.* London: LGA Publications.

Velleman, R. and Orford, J. (1999) *Risk and Resilience: Adults who were the Children of Problem Drinkers.* Harwood Academic.

Chapter 2

Reaching Out: Promoting Resilience in the Children of Substance Misusers

Richard Velleman and Lorna Templeton

Introduction

There is a huge literature (outlined below) on the negative impact that growing up with a parent with an alcohol or drug problem can have on a child, and the risk factors that can make any outcomes even worse. However, more recently an alternative way of viewing processes and outcomes for children living in such situations has been developing.

This alternative view is based on the finding that some children in these circumstances (both as children, and later as adults) do not seem to have any greater level of problems than do children who grow up in circumstances that are not disrupted by parental problematic substance misusing behaviour. They seem to be *resilient*.

This chapter will outline the evidence and the theoretical base for the emerging field of resilience, before going on to explore what practitioners can actually do to promote resilience. Most of the literature that we refer to will be from the addiction field, but we will refer, where relevant, to literature from other areas of research and practice.

Risks and negative impact

The impact of substance misuse problems (particularly alcohol and illegal drugs) on children (Gorin, 2004; Barnard and McKeganey, 2004; Kroll and Taylor, 2003; Tunnard, 2002; Harbin and Murphy, 2000; Cleaver et al., 1999) and young adults (Velleman and Orford, 1999) has been well documented (Velleman, 2004). It has been acknowledged in two key government documents, the Advisory Council on the Misuse of Drugs *Hidden Harm* report (ACMD, 2003) and the Government's Interim Analysis (Prime Minister's Strategy Unit, 2003) that preceded publication of the *National Alcohol Harm Reduction Strategy*.

Children and adolescents of people with substance misuse problems will often be at risk of developing a wide range of problems including receiving poor and neglectful parenting, having poor physical and psychological health, relationship problems, participating in unsafe sex, and having unplanned or early pregnancy. There are frequently effects on children's general education and behaviour as well. Often these problems are accompanied by a range of negative emotions such as shame, guilt, fear, anger and embarrassment. Children often have to take on extra responsibilities that are beyond their years. They often become more socially isolated, because they feel that it is too problematic or shameful to bring friends home, or because they are not able to go out with friends due to having caring responsibilities for other family members, including caring for siblings or parents who are under the influence of alcohol or drugs. They often experience or witness physical, verbal or sexual abuse. Many children affected by problem substance use within the family environment will reach the attention of social services because there are concerns regarding child protection (Forrester and Harwin, 2004). All of these issues are equally the case whether parents have alcohol or drug problems, but particular additional issues can arise when the parent misuses illicit drugs, including the illegal nature of drug misuse, the different modes of ingestion, the links to crime, the use of the home for groups of people to take drugs (with drug misuse more likely to be a home-based activity) and the links to poverty, unemployment and social deprivation.

The risks to these children, and their subsequent problems as both children and adults, have been documented and discussed (Velleman, 2004; Kroll and Taylor, 2003; Harbin and Murphy, 2000; Cleaver et al., 1999; Velleman and Orford, 1999). If unchecked, the child or young person can be at risk of any number of potential problems in all areas of life, both as young people and as adults. This includes physical and psychological ill health, difficulty in making and sustaining close relationships, a lack of confidence and low self-esteem, under achievement in education and employment, and developing the same or similar problems as experienced by the parents, including substance misuse.

Furthermore, this body of research has also demonstrated that there are some factors which have the potential to make the outcome for children even worse. These 'risk' factors have been defined as 'characteristics of the individual or the environment which increase the likelihood of a poor adaptational outcome' (Tebes et al., 2001: 116) following an event or circumstance. For the children of substance misusing parents, risk factors can include: both parents being substance misusers, substance misuse taking place in the home, the severity of the problem, the absence of a stable adult figure (such as a non-using parent, another family member or a teacher), inconsistent, ambivalent or neglectful parenting, high levels of family disharmony, including general disruption to family life, routines, rituals etc., the presence of domestic violence, parental separation or divorce, and the family not seeking help (McKeganey et al., 2002; Velleman and Orford, 1999; Cleaver et al., 1999). With particular regard to drugs, additional risk factors include: material deprivation and neglect, exposure to and awareness of criminal activity (e.g. drug dealing), presence of the child (though not necessarily in the same room) when drugs are taken, witnessing someone inject drugs and seeing paraphernalia (e.g. lying around the home) (McKeganey et al., 2002). There is a cumulative effect of these risk factors i.e. the more that are present, the higher the risk of negative outcomes.

The issues outlined above imply that the situation for these children seems somewhat bleak. It is easy to see, therefore, why many commentators have over the years thought in pessimistic ways about the future for children brought up in such an environment.

However, in recent years evidence of a rather different pattern of the impact of parental substance misuse on children has emerged. There seem to be factors and processes (for discussions on how resilience can be seen as fluid and dynamic processes, rather than static traits see, for example: Little et al., 2004; Glantz and Johnson (Eds.), 1999; Werner, 1993; Masten et al., 1990; Richardson et al., 1990; Rutter, 1987) that can minimise the negative impact of drug or alcohol problems, or even act to protect these children. It seems that not all children are adversely affected, either as children or adults (Tunnard, 2002; Cleaver et al., 1999; Velleman and Orford, 1999; Tweed and Rhyff, 1991; West and Prinz, 1987); some children are *resilient* and do not develop significant problems, or do not develop problems at any different rate to children who come from non-substance misusing families, either when they are young or when they reach adulthood and perhaps have families of their own.

Evidence for resilience

Evidence that some children do seem able to grow up in difficult circumstances without developing significant problems has been accumulating in recent years (for the most up-to-date writing in this general area see Luthar (Ed.), (2003). This book includes some chapters that relate to parental substance misuse).

Velleman and Orford (Orford and Velleman, 1990, 1995; Velleman and Orford 1990, 1993a, 1993b, 1999) conducted a unique study in the 1980s, in which 244 adults aged 16–35 years (164 were the children of problem drinkers; the remaining 80 were matched for age and recruitment source but did not have a problem drinking parent and formed a comparison group) were interviewed retrospectively and in-depth about their experiences of growing up in a family where one or both parents had an alcohol problem. Alongside the identification of risk factors for the children of problem drinkers, Velleman and Orford's research discovered that:

> . . . *many children may grow to be well functioning adults despite having experienced a very deleterious upbringing . . . [this implies that] the outlook for adult offspring is not as bleak as had been supposed, and that many of these offspring go on to make as happy and successful lives as do those without such a background.*

(246)

Similar evidence has emerged from the Kauai Longitudinal study (Werner, 1993) which followed all babies (N = 698) born in 1955 on the Hawaiian island at ages 1, 2, 10, 18 and 32. The longitudinal aspect of the study allowed for the identification of protective factors and processes in children exposed to challenging family environments as they grew up, and for some clarity to be obtained as to how these developed and changed through the life cycle. About 200 of the children were classified in a high-risk cohort typified by a disharmonious family environment (including parental 'alcoholism'). A third of this cohort:

> ... *grew into competent, confident and caring young adults. None developed serious learning or behavioural problems in childhood or adolescence . . . succeeded in school, managed home and social life well, and expressed a strong desire to take advantage of whatever opportunity came their way.*

> (Werner, 1993: 504)

Resilience and protective factors

It is useful to distinguish between protective factors or processes (which make it more likely that a child will develop resilience) and the resulting resilience factors or processes. The protective ones make it *more likely* that the child *will be able to be resilient*; the resilience ones are evidence that the child *is being resilient*. Interestingly, resilience factors and processes are also ones which make it more likely that the resilience will continue: behaving in a resilient way increases the probability of further resilient behaviour.

These protective and resilience factors and processes have been discovered in a number of different studies, both substance use specific and non-specific (e.g. Beinart et al., 2002; Werner, 1993: Velleman and Orford, 1999; Bancroft et al., 2004) (for examples of theoretical models that have been developed to explain resilience and its composite factors and process see Glantz and Johnson (Eds.), 1999; Richardson et al., 1990).

Bancroft et al.'s (2004) interview study with 37 young people aged 15–27 with parental substance misuse problems found that a number of protective factors could lead to more resilient outcomes, including positive input from school, immediate family, siblings, extended family and individuals/services external to the family. It should not be thought, however, that such positive input was easy to maintain! Whilst young people in this study stated that some positive input from immediate and extended family was obtainable and was certainly beneficial, they also stated that longer-term, unconditional support was rare, and certainly nowhere near the levels needed or desired by these young people. Other strategies employed by the young people in this study included escaping (spending time in their room or going out e.g. to visit friends) and challenging the user (although this latter was rarely successful). In common with findings from other research (e.g. Velleman and Orford, 1999) moving on from these difficult pasts could be helped by the young people having goals and dreams and then by making them happen, utilising education or work opportunities, moving away, and developing their own future via their own family, children etc. A central issue was the young person feeling that they had choices and were in control of their lives.

A list of the protective factors gleaned from these studies outlined or referenced above includes:

- The presence of a stable adult figure (usually a non-problem drinker).
- Close positive bond with at least one adult in a caring role (include parents, siblings and grandparents).
- A good support network beyond this.
- Low separation from the primary carer in the first year of life.
- Characteristics and care style of parents.
- Being raised in a small family.
- Larger age gaps between siblings.
- Engagement in a range of activities.
- Individual temperament.
- Positive opportunities at times of life transition.
- Further, much research shows that, if family cohesion and harmony can be maintained in the face of substance misuse (or domestic violence or mental illness), then there is a high chance that the child will not go on to have any problems (Cleaver et al., 1999; Velleman and Orford, 1999).

A list of the resilience factors or processes which these protective factors encouraged includes:

- Deliberate planning by the child that their adult life would be different.
- High self-esteem and confidence.
- Self-efficacy.
- An ability to deal with change.
- Skills and values that lead to efficient use of personal ability.
- A good range of problem solving skills.
- The young person feeling that they had choices.
- The young person feeling that they were in control of their lives.
- Previous experience of success and achievement.

The key issue for resilience is the overcoming of psychological risk (Rutter, 1987). The protective factors make it more likely that this risk will be able to be overcome by providing a more positive setting for the child. The resilience factors make it more likely by providing a set of skills and feelings in the child that enable it to be forward looking, and to bounce back from adversity.

It is also clear that developmental changes and stages, and the interaction with other factors (such as gender, temperament, parent-child relationships, marital support, planning, school experiences, early parental loss) at key transition points in life, can have a particular impact on the development of resilience (Cleaver et al., 1999; Werner, 1993; Rutter, 1987).

Is resilience always positive?

A few notes of caution must be sounded in relation to the resilience findings. All strategies have potential risks associated with them; their success or levels of benefit are by no means guaranteed. This means that the processes which allow young people to become resilient may not all be totally positive, either in the short- or the long-term.

For example, some researchers (e.g. Bancroft et al., 2004; Kroll and Taylor, 2003; Velleman and Orford, 1999) have noted that certain strategies that may be beneficial and effective when younger, may be more harmful in the longer-term when older. For example, strategies of detachment, avoidance and withdrawal, such as those noted by Werner and Johnson (1999) who described detachment by some children especially from: 'family members whose domestic and emotional problems threaten to engulf them', are often very effective when used by a powerless child in dealing with substance misusing parents. However, these same strategies can lead to problems with attachment and relationships when these children grow older. Along the same lines, in an earlier report Werner (1993) noticed that some of her sample were detached from things and people: 'they had learned to keep the memories of their childhood adversities at bay by being in the world but not of it'. For some, the skills they have learnt which allow them to be resilient can have negative sides, particularly in relationships with others. Learning to get on with one's own life may in some people also lead to them being seen as aloof or detached.

Some protective strategies are also less possible for some people. Hence although the research outlined above has found that support from friends is an important protective factor for young people, this is often balanced by the fact that the same research has shown that many individuals in this situation, particularly younger children, found it hard to make friends. Similarly, although many young people tended to leave home earlier than they otherwise might have done, wanting to escape and try to achieve their own independence, adulthood and normality, a number of these young people were left feeling that they had lost their childhood and youth, and some were at risk for developing their own problems (with substances, early pregnancy, housing difficulties etc.).

What can practitioners actually do?

This chapter has shown that there is clear evidence that some children are resilient, and that there are identifiable factors that seem to be associated with both the protection of children and the promotion of resilience and a resilient outcome.

But can practitioners do anything to promote these outcomes? We argue here that there are two clear ways whereby practitioners can help to promote resilience:

- They can work to reduce the risks for and to children (the fewer risk factors, the more likely it is that children will not be negatively affected).

- They can work to increase the protective processes and factors (the more of them there are, the more likely it is that children will be resilient).

Clearly both of these activities will involve not just the child, but the family and possibly wider social networks.

Reducing risk

All the things which are major risk factors are amenable to intervention, even if the parental substance misuse is not, at this time. As we outlined above, the major risk factors relate to issues within the family, as opposed to the drinking or drug-taking per se. This means that practitioners working with families where parents have substance misuse problems, if they wish to reduce risk, need to work on:

- Family disharmony and, within this, on:
  – family violence;
  – parental conflict;
  – parental separation and loss;
  – inconsistent and ambivalent parenting.

It is these things that seem to pose a greater risk for the short and long-term well being of children than the substance misuse problem itself. And all can be worked on, using the skills and techniques (conflict resolution, anger management, couple counselling) that are available in most practitioners' kitbags.

Increasing protective factors and resilience

The second way that practitioners can help to promote resilience is to work on the protective and the resilience factors and processes. We have shown above that some of the elements that make up resilience in children are now understood. So again, we can work with families to develop these characteristics.

As far as *protective factors and processes* are concerned, we can work with:

- *The other parent*, enabling them to provide a stable environment and give the time and attention which so many children require.
- *The parental relationship*, enabling parents to retain their cohesive relationship and present a united and caring front to the children.
- *The family relationship*, ensuring that family *relationships*, family *affection*, and family *activities* are maintained.
- *Other adult figures outside of the nuclear family*, ensuring that there is at least someone who can provide the necessary stabilising influence.

For many professionals this work might involve direct intervention with other key adult figures, e.g. grandparents, teachers, parents. A finding from a qualitative study of 62 drug using parents in Scotland (Barnard, 2003: 298) found 'the level and extent of the extended family's involvement in caring for children and supporting parents' to be pivotal to the well-being of the child. Most importantly, they found that there was a clear correlation where, if such support was not present, the child was more likely to be 'looked after' (i.e. taken into local authority care).

These factors within a child's environment will mean that they are more protected, and hence more likely to develop resilience. The task for practitioners, therefore, is to enable children and young people to develop these resilience factors (see below). Essentially, within the remit of a professional role which will dictate their level of contact with, and responsibility towards, a child, practitioners can utilise this relatively basic knowledge of protective factors and processes to contribute towards the child's development of resilience. The practitioner needs to work with *the child* itself, enabling the child to:

- Maintain the positive family rituals within the family.
- Remove themselves from the disruptive behaviour of the problem parent or parents.
- Disengage from the disruptive elements of family life.
- Engage with stabilising others outside the family.
- Engage with stabilising activities (school, clubs, sports, culture, religion etc.) within which the child can develop a sense of self and self-esteem.

The key task for developing resilience, then, is to help a child to identify and build on their strengths, including the social support they can call on, enabling them to build meaning and motivation into their lives, helping them to acquire social skills that bring self-control, self-esteem and a sense of humour (Little, Axford and Morpeth, 2004), and helping them reframe negative events and emotions into positive ones, such that better life decisions are made.

Interventions need to take into account the age, gender and developmental level of the child. For example, younger children will not be so able to seek external support due to issues of needing transport, money, forms signed, issues of protection and safety and so on. Girls seem less affected by parental problem drinking in the short-term but if the situation continues then there is an increased likelihood of problems developing (see Cleaver et al., 1999). Werner (1993) also found that the 'individual disposition' was more important for females, whereas external support was more important for males. Boys feel that conflict is more of a threat to them, whilst girls appraise the conflict in terms of how it affects them, and are more likely to blame themselves (Reynolds, 2001). The setting in which the intervention is undertaken can also be important. This work does not need to be conducted in individual counselling or case-work, there is evidence that a group approach can be effective in promoting resilience in young people who have experienced stressful backgrounds (including but not solely related to parental substance misuse) (Waaktaar et al., 2004).

What skills are needed for practitioners to do this work?

Many child care practitioners tell us that they cannot work with parents with alcohol or drug problems in order to reduce risk factors or increase protective ones, and that they do not have the skills to do this. Strangely, many alcohol and drug practitioners tell us the converse in that they do not have the skills to work with children and the wider family in order to do the same things. Our response is the same to both.

The key idea here is that all practitioners use *the same basic skills* of therapeutic relationship formation and counselling (Velleman, 2001). Working with children and other family members needs the same skills as working with people with substance misuse problems. For all work with people (adults or children) you need to:

- Be warm, empathic and genuine.
- Make a therapeutic relationship.
- Help clients explore their difficulties.
- Enable clients to set achievable goals.
- Empower clients to take action to reach these achievable goals.
- Stay with clients and help them to stabilise and maintain changes.

Clearly sometimes, especially with younger children, you need to apply these skills slightly differently, or alongside other skills, such as through using art or play; but the essential skill base remains the same. Overall, these are the same skills, irrespective of the age of the person with whom one is working, or the number of people present in the room.

Promoting resilience within child social work

In the particular field of child social work, two guides have been produced to support practitioners in promoting resilience (Newman, 2002; Gilligan, 2000). Whilst not directly written for practitioners who work with children who have experienced parental substance misuse, there is much within both documents that is useful for professionals who are working with, or come into contact with, children who are or have been in such a situation. And because both guides build on some of the ideas that we have raised in this chapter, they can be applied relatively easily to the more specialist area of working with the children of parents with alcohol or drug problems.

The Newman publication is a review of the evidence and work to date in this area, as well as summarising key strategies and interventions that exist to support professionals who wish to try and incorporate a resilience element to their work with children and young people. Usefully, this book looks at how such work can be undertaken in the early years, in middle childhood, in adolescence, and in early adulthood, thus highlighting the importance of life transition points and the potential for particular interventions at these times.

Newman also provides a brief summary of the work and evidence that is available for working with children who have parents with alcohol problems, highlighting one of the points made above. A key finding from the research is that promoting a safe and stable family environment (maintaining family roles and rituals etc., ensuring family harmony) is a vital protective factor. Other points that Newman makes are that having 'activities and confidants' outside the family as well as a desire to be, and pride in being, a survivor, are all protective factors. These protective factors are likely to lead to resilience in children, with corresponding longer-term benefits for the adolescent and young adult.

The Gilligan guide on working in the care system views resilience as a process, not something internal to the individual that needs to be promoted. Gilligan suggests that interactions with self, others and the environment need to be taken into account (see also, for example, Kumpfer, 1999) and viewed also in the wider context of child development. Gilligan suggests focussing on the following: the importance of social roles, having a secure base, identity (knowing their own story), self-esteem and self-efficacy, as well as working to uphold the relationships that children and young people have with key figures in their lives, and ensuring that the child or young person can make the most out of opportunities and experiences (with particular reference to education and leisure). The guide also looks at the role that key adults have to play, such as carers, mentors, social workers and other professionals.

Policy developments and the assessment framework

Although there is some work underway, based on the ideas outlined above, there is a need for the development of these approaches in the specific area of working with children and other family members where there is parental substance misuse.

Resilience is developing as a concept and is becoming more of a feature of theory, research, practice and policy. The *Looking After Children* initiative (Flynn et al., 2004), and the *Assessment and Action Record* (described by Flynn et al., 2004), are both examples of developments in this field.

The most notable example of policy development in this area is the *Framework for the Assessment of Children in Need and their Families* (Department of Health, 2000), which has three domains of assessment (based to a large extent on the work of Cleaver et al., 1999):

- *Parenting capacity:* This includes basic care, ensuring safety, emotional warmth, stimulation, guidance and boundaries, and stability.
- *Family and environmental factors:* This includes community resources, social integration, income, employment, housing, wider family, and family history and functioning.
- *The child's developmental needs:* This includes health, education, emotional and behavioural development, identity, family and social relationships, social presentation, and self-care skills.

Commentary on the *Assessment Framework* has highlighted that:

> *In the past, assessments of children in need led by social services had tended to focus primarily on issues of abuse and neglect in that they were incident driven rather than adopting a holistic focus that identified children's developmental needs and circumstances.*
>
> (Cleaver and Walker, 2004: 81)

Thus, the *Framework* was developed to offer such an holistic, multi-agency approach in considering the 'full range of children's and family's strengths as well as needs and difficulties, including the wider environment and circumstances in which they live' (Cleaver and Walker, 2004: 82).

Cleaver and Walker (2004) looked at the impact of the *Framework* in terms of social work assessments in 24 English councils and their impact on implementation and practice, finding that good progress has been made with the implementation of the *Framework*, and which has been welcomed by staff at all levels and been seen as an ideal opportunity to review current policy and practice and change for the better:

> *. . . (it) provided a foundation for strengthening the assessment of children in need and their families . . . Framework has contributed to an increase in the involvement of children and families at all levels of the assessment process.*
>
> (88)

Murphy and Harbin (2000) have suggested that there be a fourth domain to the *Assessment Framework*, one that looks at the use of the substance (taking into account such factors as what substance, how much is taken or obtained, how is the substance ingested, what is the pattern of use, where is the substance taken and with whom, what is the cost of the substance use and what are the implications for lifestyle). Also, the links between the substance use and parenting, the effects on the child's needs and child care demands, and thus ultimately, the impact on the child. This additional domain would therefore integrate in one process the work of both substance misuse and child and social care practitioners, which would also serve to overcome the barriers to information sharing and confidentiality that exist in this arena. Indeed, this idea could be extended further, so that the measurement and assessment of both risk and protective factors and processes (i.e. the presence of elements which potentially could be used to build resilience) could form a fifth domain, or an extension of each of the existing domains of the *Framework* (with or without the addition of Murphy and Harbins's substance use domain).

Resilience versus deficits

Historically, theory, practice and research in health and social care have been preoccupied with illness, vulnerability and the pathology of life's problems (Richardson et al., 1990). More recently (Flynn et al., 2004) there has been a growing interest in 'positive psychology', which is more preoccupied with health and well being, and the positive aspect of life's problems, of what 'keeps people healthy, rather than what makes them sick' (Newman, 2002). This shift has included the emergence of the concept of resilience, both as a philosophical approach, and as a practical way of understanding and working with people affected by problems.

Until recently, deficit models that focused on risk and negative short and long-term outcomes were the dominant way for thinking about the impact that substance misuse has on children and young people. This developing concept of 'resilience' is part of a broader shift in thinking, seen particularly with the emergence of the field of 'positive psychology', which has been defined as 'the potential for positive change through trauma and suffering' (Linley, 2000: 353). Linley highlights research that has demonstrated positive adaptation following 'trauma', events that include the sinking of a cruise-ship, cancer, heart attack, victims of a lightning strike, survivors of sexual abuse or of childhood sexual abuse. Similar findings have emerged following major incidents such as the Paddington rail disaster and terrorist attacks such as those in New York, Bali and Madrid. There are links to PTSD (post-traumatic stress disorder), with researchers and clinicians discovering how traumas such as those can result in what has been termed 'post-traumatic growth' (Linley, 2000).

Resilience theory contrasts with genetic theories which posit that the children of substance misusing parents are at particular and specific risk of developing behavioural and substance misuse problems of their own, and co-dependent theories, which state that the 'children of alcoholics and addicts' are particularly affected by a parental substance misuse problem, that they will suffer particular and significant problems when they are children, and are at particular risk of developing problems in adulthood, most likely problems with substances and relationships, even entering into damaging relationships with people with substance misuse problems.

Conceptually, resilience is important because it implies that some children, even if they live in disadvantageous circumstances, either are resilient, or have the capacity to become so. This implies that it is not a foregone conclusion that all children who live in such circumstances are, or will be, damaged. This has major implications for both intervention and policy. It suggests that intervention with children who live in difficult circumstances should not wait until a crisis is reached and damage is apparent. Neither should intervention focus solely on reducing risk factors. Instead, it implies that there is much that can be done earlier in life to promote factors associated with greater resilience, and to encourage the development of resilience in children who are at increased risk of experiencing greater problems. As Werner (1993) argued:

> ... our examination of the long-term effects of childhood adversity and of protective factors and processes in the lives of high-risk youths has shown that some of the most critical determinants of adult outcomes are present in the first decade of life.

(513)

Waiting for problems to occur often makes offering help more difficult. There are many policy implications here, for greater and earlier preventative interventions.

However, it is also important to recognise that most people deal with adversity on a greater or smaller scale on a daily basis. Few of us lead such cushioned lives that we do not experience challenges and change in our lives. This realisation has led some commentators to ask what is so unique about resilience. Some have answered this by suggesting that what makes resilience different is that the scale of adversity is such that 'part of the essential character of 'resilience' seems to be that the positive outcome was unexpected . . . a model or theory fails to accurately predict behaviour for some individuals' (Glantz and Sloboda, 1999: 113). Hence the suggestion would be that the level of difficulty that many children of those with serious substance use problems face is such that theory would predict that they should develop problems in turn.

Others have suggested that resilience is a basic human facility, which may get lost in some individuals due to the depth of problems within their circumstances, problems which lead to a loss of confidence and of self-esteem, such that these natural resilience processes cannot easily be instituted. This idea suggests that the capacity for resilience is within us all; it just gets hidden sometimes, and needs teasing out for some people. Sometimes these people whose resilience is hidden are people who are living in particular adversity; but sometimes it is hidden as these people are not called upon to show resilience: perhaps because trauma or adversity is not such a central feature in their lives.

For example, in Bancroft et al.'s (2004) sample, resilience did not necessarily mean growing up or being stronger, but:

> . . . *involved creating space to focus on themselves and their needs, and to have fun, without responsibilities for others . . . they were often having to relearn, or learn for the first time, the joys and pleasures of being young, or being able focus on themselves and their own needs.*

(78)

Getting it right in youth can be beneficial when older, as resilience, much like other things (traits, characteristics) is something that is fluid to change through childhood, but starts to stabilise through adolescence and adulthood: if you get it right earlier, you are more likely to keep it right. Flynn et al. (2004) wrote that:

> . . . *(these) foregoing protective factors are, in fact, but concrete manifestations of more basic human adaptational systems that promote positive behavioural development or that, when adversity occurs, facilitate resilience.*

(66)

Thus, personal or clinical interventions to build resilience may not need to be concerned with developing something unusual, they may be more concerned with enabling young people to develop something which is inherent within the human system. Interventions therefore may be more about raising awareness over the possibilities of resilience, and putting into place strategies for promoting such resilience.

Conclusion

This chapter has argued that it is relatively clear how professionals can help families to reduce risk, develop protective factors, and promote resilience in young people. Further work is needed to encourage and train professionals to work in a more focused and integrated way, looking at the full range of a child's needs within a broader context, including working within such a protective, resilience framework. Our emphasis here is that:

- Practitioners *can* intervene.
- The focus does not have to be on the substance misuse problem, but on providing necessary beneficial factors in children's lives.
- Practitioners must not be sidetracked into focusing on parental problems, but must instead focus on the child's needs and how to meet them.

References

Advisory Council on the Misuse of Drugs (2003) *Hidden Harm: Responding to the Needs of Children of Problem Drug Users*. ACMD.

Bancroft, A. et al. (2004) *Risk and Resilience: Older Children of Drug and Alcohol Misusing Parents*. Final Report to the Joseph Rowntree Foundation.

Barnard, M. and McKeganey, N. (2004) The Impact of Parental Problem Drug Use on Children: What is the Problem and What can be done to Help? *Addiction*. 99: 5, 552–9.

Barnard, M. (1999) Forbidden Questions: Drug Dependent Parents and the Welfare of their Children. *Addiction*. 94: 8, 1109–11.

Barnard, M. (2003) Between a Rock and a Hard Place: The Role of Relatives in Protecting Children from the Effects of Parental Drug Problems. *Child and Family Social Work*. 8: 291–9.

Beinart, S., Anderson, B., Lee, S. and Utting, D. (2002) *Youth at Risk? A National Survey of Risk Factors, Protective Factors and Problem Behaviour among Young People in England, Scotland and Wales*. London: Communities that Care; JRF Findings 432.

Cleaver, H. and Walker, S. (2004) From Policy to Practice: The Implementation of a New Framework for Social Work Assessments of Children and Families. *Child and Family Social Work*. 9: 81–90.

Cleaver, H., Unel, I. and Aldgate, J. (1999) *Children's Needs: Parenting Capacity*. London: HMSO.

Department of Health, Department for Education and Employment, Home Office (2000) *Framework for the Assessment of Children in Need and their Families*. London: The Stationery Office.

Flynn, R.J. et al. (2004) Use of Population Measures and Norms to Identify Resilient Outcomes in Young People in Care: An Exploratory Study. *Child and Family Social Work*. 9: 65–79.

Forrester, D. and Harwin, J. (2004) Social Work and Parental Substance Misuse. In Phillips, R. (Ed.) *Children Exposed to Parental Substance Misuse: Implications for Family Placement.* London: BAAF.

Gilligan, R. (2000) *Promoting Resilience: A Resource Guide on Working with Children in the Care System.* London: BAAF.

Glantz, M.D. and Johnson, J.L. (Eds.) (1999) *Resilience and Development: Positive Life Adaptations.* New York: Kluwer Academic/Plenum Publishers.

Glantz, M.D. and Sloboda, Z. (1999) Analysis and Re-conceptualization of Resilience. In Glantz, M.D. and Johnson, J.L. (Eds.) (1999) *Resilience and Development: Positive Life Adaptations.* New York: Kluwer Academic/Plenum Publishers.

Gorin, S. (2004) *Understanding what Children Say. Children's Experiences of Domestic Violence, Parental Substance Misuse and Parental Health Problems.* London: NCB.

Harbin, F. and Murphy, M. (2000) (Eds.) *Substance Misuse and Child Care: How to Understand, Assist and Intervene when Drugs Affect Parenting.* Lyme Regis: Russell House Publishing.

Kroll, B. and Taylor, A. (2003) *Parental Substance Misuse and Child Welfare.* London: Jessica Kingsley.

Kumpfer, K.L. (1999) Factors and Processes Contributing to Resilience: The Resilience Framework. In Glantz, M.D. and Johnson, J.L. (Eds.) (1999) *Resilience and Development: Positive Life Adaptations.* New York: Kluwer Academic/Plenum Publishers.

Linley, A. (2000) Transforming Psychology: The Example of Trauma. *The Psychologist.* 13: 7, 353–5.

Little, M., Axford, N. and Morpeth, L. (2004) Research Review: Risk and Protection in the Context of Services for Children in Need. *Child and Family Social Work.* 9: 105–17.

Luthar, S.S. (Ed.) (2003) *Resilience and Vulnerability: Adaptation in the Context of Childhood Adversities.* Cambridge: Cambridge University Press.

Masten, A.S., Best, K.M. and Garmezy, N. (1990) Resilience and Development: Contributions from the Study of Children who Overcome Adversity. *Development and Psychopathology* 2: 425–44.

McKeganey, N., Barnard, M. and McIntosh, J. (2002) Paying the Price for their Parents' Addiction: Meeting the Needs of the Children of Drug-using Parents. *Drugs: Education, Prevention and Policy.* 9: 3, 233–46.

Murphy, M. and Harbin, F. (2000) Background and Current Context of Substance Misuse and Child Care. In Harbin, F. and Murphy, M. (2000) (Eds.) *Substance Misuse and Child Care: How to Understand, Assist and Intervene when Drugs Affect Parenting.* Lyme Regis: Russell House Publishing.

Newman, T. (2002) *Promoting Resilience: A Review of Effective Strategies for Child Care Services.* Exeter: Centre for Evidence-based Social Services, and Barnado's.

Orford, J. and Velleman, R. (1995) Childhood and Adulthood Influences on the Adjustment of Young Adults with and without Parents with Drinking Problems. *Addiction Research.* 3, 1–15.

Orford, J. and Velleman, R. (1990) Offspring of Parents with Drinking Problems: Drinking and Drug-taking as Young Adults. *British Journal of Addiction.* 85, 779–94.

Prime Minister's Strategy Unit (2003) *National Alcohol Harm Reduction Strategy.* Interim Analysis.

Reynolds, J. (2001) *Not in Front of the Children: How Conflict between Parents Affects Children.* One plus One Marriage and Partnership Research.

Richardson, G.E. et al. (1990) The Resiliency Model. *Health Education.* 21: 6, 33–9.

Rutter, M. (1987) Psychosocial Resilience and Protective Mechanisms. *American Journal of Orthopsychiatry.* 57: 3, 316–31.

Tebes, J.K. et al. (2001) Resilience and Family Psychosocial Processes among Children of Parents with Serious Mental Disorders. *Journal of Child and Family Studies.* 10: 1, 115–36.

Tunnard, J. (2002) *Research in Practice: Parental Problem Drinking and its Impact on Children.* Research in Practice.

Tweed, S.H. and Rhyff, C.D. (1991) Adult Children of Alcoholics: Profiles of Wellness amidst Distress. *Journal of Studies on Alcohol.* 52: 2, 133–41.

Velleman, R. (2001) *Counselling for Alcohol Problems.* London: Sage.

Velleman, R. (2004) Alcohol and Drug Problems in Parents: An Overview of the Impact on Children and Implications for Practice. In Gopfert, M., Webster, J. and Seeman, M.V. (2004) (Eds.) *Seriously Disturbed and Mentally Ill Parents and their Children.* 2nd Ed. Cambridge University Press.

Velleman, R. and Orford, J. (1990) Young Adult Offspring of Parents with Drinking Problems: Recollections of Parents' Drinking and its Immediate Effects. *British Journal of Clinical Psychology.* 29: 297–317.

Velleman, R. and Orford, J. (1993a) The Importance of Family Discord in Explaining Childhood Problems in the Children of Problem Drinkers. *Addiction Research.* 1, 39–57.

Velleman, R. and Orford, J. (1993b) The Adulthood Adjustment of Offspring of Parents with Drinking Problems. *British Journal of Psychiatry.* 162, 503–16.

Velleman, R. and Orford, J. (1999) *Risk and Resilience: Adults Who Were the Children of Problem Drinkers.* Harwood Academic.

Waaktaar, T. et al. (2004) How Can Young People's Resilience be Enhanced? Experiences from a Clinical Intervention Project. *Clinical Child Psychology and Psychiatry.* 9: 2, 167–83.

Werner, E. (1993) Risk, Resilience and Recovery: Perspectives from the Kauai Longitudinal Study. *Development and Psychopathology.* 5, 503–15.

Werner, E. and Johnson, J.L. (1999) Can we Apply Resilience? In Glantz, M.D. and Johnson, J.L. (Eds.) *Resilience and Development: Positive Life Adaptations.* New York: Kluwer Academic/Plenum Publishers.

West, M.O. and Prinz, R.J. (1987) Parental Alcoholism and Childhood Psychopathology. *Psychological Bulletin.* 102: 2, 204–18.

Chapter 3

Using Group Work to Support Young People Living with Substance Misuse

Ellen Wheeler

> Practitioner: *What would you like to call this group?*
> Child (9 years old): *Secret Lives, because we can talk about what is really going on at home.*

Introduction

This chapter investigates group work support for children and young people who live with substance misuse in their families. Not only the substance misuse of their parents but, in many cases, the substance misuse of their siblings and extended family. Group work is one model of intervention that has worked particularly well for most of the children and young people who joined groups in our area. It is one of several interventions used in a needs-led approach to service provision.

The setting

The support groups were run by Project 360, an under 19s substance misuse service for young people and their families. Project 360 is a multi-agency and interdisciplinary team, funded jointly by Bolton Drug Action Team, Bolton Primary Health Care Trust, Bolton Social Services, and the Youth Justice Board and managed by Bolton Social Services Children and Families Division. The aim of the young people's substance misuse service is to identify and intervene early with young people and their families on issues of substance misuse and substance related problems. The service offers a range of education, prevention, treatment and rehabilitation for children and young people, with a family support provision for the whole family (see Chapter 10). The service takes a holistic approach to substance misuse, addressing not only the substance itself, but also the general social, psychological, and physical well being of the young people referred.

The need for a service

It became evident at an early stage in the project's life, that there was a need to offer the siblings of young people involved in the project a service to look at early preventative work and intervention. The project's statistics identified that there were second and third generation substance users accessing our service. There was a service for the substance user, support for their parents and families, but nothing specific for their younger siblings who were also experiencing the impact of substance misuse on their families.

Research suggests that the impact of parental substance misuse is a significant contributory factor in some young people's misuse (Velleman and Orford, 1999; Hoffman and Su, 1998). Our own experience and research (Kearney et al., 2005: Ch. 9) identified that a significant minority of young people were being introduced to substances by their older siblings.

Previously Bolton ACPC had sponsored a group for young people whose parents were misusing substances (Harbin, 2000). This group had worked predominantly with young people who were already within child protection or looked after systems, with most of the participants living away from their parents (see Chapter 4). The nature of the work at the young people's service meant that the children and young people identified were often assessed as being in need but not necessarily in need of protection. This very different group of young people were often living at home with their parent/s and had had no previous contact with child care agencies. This was to be a distinctly different group from those we had already run.

Why a group?

Bolton child care system had already positively evaluated groups for young people living with substance misusing parents, and recognised the potential benefits for young people still living in families with substance problems (Harbin, 2000). Group work has been recognised as a beneficial intervention in many areas of people work. Group attendance can:

- Provide access to the experiences of the other group members.
- Provide a forum for creativity.
- Often be more fun than individual work.
- Help to reduce feelings of isolation through knowledge that others may have shared similar experiences.
- Provide a structured setting for members to express their own concerns and feelings.
- Provide a forum for diffusing the sense of shame and stigma that the children of drug using parents may feel.

For this group of children, in particular, group attendance can offer confirmation and affirmation that their experiences are not exceptional. A group can provide a safe environment to practice new life skills and social interactions. It is frightening for children not to be able to talk about what is happening at home, yet talking to parents about their concerns is often too difficult (Kearney et al., 2005). Children need to feel that they can check out their emotional and physical responses to substance misuse in the family in order to reassure themselves that their responses are normal. The group can provide this opportunity in a way that other interventions cannot. A group can also provide the context for helping young people build up resilience. Gilligan (2001) describes resilience as the qualities which cushion a vulnerable child from the worst effects of adversity. However, in order to be truly effective resilience requires a positive social context and a group can, if well run, become a significant provider of this context.

However, there are circumstances which may hinder group work and may inhibit its benefits. Group work can only take place if there is a group of similar people needing similar support at a similar time. Experience predicts that this is not always the case and attempts to run more diverse groups, for example with a wide age range have not always been successful (Harbin, 2000).

The support and agreement of the parent or carer for the young person's attendance at the group is also essential. Parents, unsurprisingly, recognise that a group entails their child disclosing information about their home life and in many situations about their substance misuse. This can evoke a fear that family secrets will be revealed, and their children will be taken from them (Kearney and Taylor, 2001).

The timing of a group is also vital. Group work is not always the most appropriate intervention at all times for all children. Many children and young people living with substance misuse in their family may not wish to attend a group for many reasons. Some children may not feel comfortable in a group setting, and may prefer individual interventions. Some young people may not wish to attend because of fears about confidentiality, especially when the child lives in a community where substance misuse is common and other participants may be neighbours or peers.

It may be possible to work through these issues. To help pre-empt any possible problems, consideration of the following factors, in the planning stage, are important:

- A thorough assessment of the needs and development of the young person.
- The young person's views on attendance at a group.
- Parental consent and understanding of their supportive role during and after the group.
- Clear explanation of the aims, objectives and group content to the parents and carers, to aid their decision making.
- Ongoing concurrent support for parents and carers.
- Consideration of individual work with the young person.
- Consideration of group work at a later date.
- Consideration of the most appropriate workers to facilitate and manage the group.

Structural and organisational aspects of the group

There are many organisational practicalities which must be addressed before any group can run. These often seem quite unrelated to the therapeutic aims of the group, but good organisation at this stage can help the smooth running of the therapeutic interventions at a later stage.

Funding

Many groups can be run and funded by mainstream services and can be accommodated in existing budgets. However, there is a view that by packing more children into the group you are choosing a cheaper option. This soon reveals itself as a myth. Group work often takes more planning, more debriefing, and support for the young person and their family away from the group is essential. Transport costs, equipment and refreshments have also to be budgeted for, so some supplementary funding is often required. In our area the Children's Fund provided some financial assistance, and the Communities against Drugs Fund also helped to fund the intervention. The early intervention with this vulnerable group fits the objectives of the government's Updated Drug Strategy (2002), which in turn makes the intervention more attractive to sponsors.

Group facilitators

Our groups were not facilitated by 'specialists' in group work practice. Instead, practitioners with a genuine interest and expertise in working with children, with a basic knowledge of substances and an understanding of child development, ran the groups. Their most essential trait is an enthusiasm and a commitment to working with children in groups.

Facilitators from different settings within a child care service can share experience and techniques which can benefit the process. The number of facilitators can depend on the size of the group, but our experience indicated that there should be at least two even in a very small group. Co-working offers the advantages of task sharing, joint preparation, feedback, planning, liaison and comparing observation and evaluation (Dwidevi, 1993).

Access and referral

Referrals to the group come from anyone concerned about a child or young person living with parental or sibling substance misuse. Initially, referrals were predominantly from the young person's substance misuse project, but gradually referrals came from adult substance misuse services, social services, and children themselves (often via school nurses). All the young people were assessed as children in need of a service because they were living in a household where substance misuse was perceived to be a problem.

Initial assessment

Initial assessments of the children and their families were undertaken to ascertain if they would benefit from the programme. This initial assessment gave the group facilitators an overview of:

- Substances used in the home.
- Treatment being offered to the sibling or parent.
- The young person's level of knowledge about substances, and, most importantly,
- How this substance misuse was impacting on the young person.

The assessments used the guidance of *The Framework for the Assessment of Children in Need and their Families* (DoH, 2000) with help from the more detailed assessment on parental substance misuse outlined by Harbin and Murphy (2003).

Written consent from the children, parents and carers was required so that the work could be evaluated and researched. Agreements on confidentiality were discussed and signed, and workers clarified at what point it would be necessary to share concerns and information with other professionals. This was all accomplished within the boundaries of Bolton's 'Child Concern Model' (Jones and O'Loughlin, 2003).

Allaying parental anxiety

Substance misuse is an extremely emotive issue. For many reasons, families may not wish it to be discussed outside the home. Substance misuse is often covered in a veil of secrecy and taboo. To allow your son or daughter to attend a group specifically aimed at children living with substance misuse, is a significant step for many parents. Their fears were two-fold:

- Firstly, a fear that information shared in the group would lead to them being criticised as a parent and their children being removed.
- Secondly, they feared that the group would provide explicit information on substances and how to use them.

To allay these anxieties parents and young people were engaged in a sensitive way. Clear information was given about our aims and objectives and we emphasised this was a therapeutic support group, rather than an assessment group. The need for the siblings and sons and daughters of users to have support and appropriate information was highlighted. This could ensure that the young people were not misinformed or left with unanswered questions. Offering home visits to reassure families about the project helped them to overcome their fears about the group. This was particularly important for those parents who felt that their children had been shielded from parental or sibling drug use.

Parents and carers were reassured that any educational work done on substances would be based on the key stages outlined in the DfES guidance. There would, however, be an extra focus on substances being used within the home and any substance related questions put by the young people themselves would be answered honestly in an age appropriate way.

Each young person and parent was asked what they knew about the drug use in their household.

Practice Scenario 1

Parent: *No, they don't know much about what's going on – they don't know that their sister is taking heroin.*

Worker: *Shall we ask them what they know? Do you know why your sister is involved with us and having treatment?*

Child: *Yes, she's using smack.*

Parents were often shocked at the level of knowledge that their children had about the current situation, and were usually happy to allow them to access the project. Following discussion there was generally little resistance or major concern expressed by parents. The group was not perceived as a threat. The majority of parents were keen for their children to come to a group and be given information around substances. Some believed it might prevent them from suffering the effects of drug use in later life.

The setting of the group within the young people's substance misuse service appeared more acceptable to those who were referred, whereas previous groups within a child protection setting had not been so readily accepted.

Compatibility

Care was taken to ensure the compatibility of the group so that activities could meet the needs of all those involved. Previous experience had shown that an incompatible group could inhibit the therapeutic aim. Age, gender, culture, ethnicity and the developmental levels of the young people were also considered. It was agreed that the groups would be of mixed gender with an age range from 8–13 years old.

Aims and objectives of the group

Aim

The aim of the group was to provide early supportive intervention and prevention work for vulnerable young people at risk of substance misuse.

Objectives

- To raise awareness around substances and treatment so that informed choices could be made.

- To allow the participants the opportunity to put substance misuse into a wider context.
- To enable the participants to explore perceptions of substance use and its effects.
- To allow the participants to express themselves and share their experiences in a safe environment.
- To provide a group experience that demonstrates that the young people are not alone in their situation.
- To provide messages for practice.
- To engage a disadvantaged group of young people into mainstream services.

Demographic features of the participants

Seven groups were facilitated between 2000 and 2001. Each group consisted of up to six young people. Over the two years the participants were 38 per cent male and 62 per cent female and came from backgrounds of varying degrees of need and concern. One third were living with sibling substance misuse, whilst almost three quarters were living with parental substance misuse, with a smaller number living in households where they were experiencing both parental and sibling misuse.

The majority (59 per cent) of the young people were still living with one or both parents. Of those living with alternative carers 16 per cent were living with grandparents. Only 6 per cent were in the looked after system or living with foster carers. Many young people were assessed at level 2 to 3 vulnerability on our Child Concern Model. This meant that they were receiving multi-agency support, but they were not predominantly a group who had been placed on the child protection register or been assessed as in need of protection.

Group endings and evaluation

The facilitators evaluated each session by debrief sessions and write-ups. The children were also asked to evaluate each session with easy to read questions, asking them for likes, dislikes and if there was anything they wanted to speak about. Most of the comments from the children and young people were favourable. They reported the group as having been a safe and comfortable environment to share some of their experiences and build up relationships with other young people in a similar situation.

The young people who attended the group were recognised as being vulnerable in many different ways, but specifically that of misusing substances themselves. Whilst this is difficult to measure in the short term, it was significant that of the children who participated in the group only three were re-referred to the service as problem users themselves. In the same period six young people who were referred to the group but did not attend, were re-referred as problem users.

An exit strategy was developed for the end of the groups. For many of the young people it was their only support or form of structured social activities. A routine had been established and new relationships had been formed with relatively hard to reach young people. In order to maintain the progress made, links were made with a local charitable organisation that provided social activities and events out of school. Funding was used to continue the transport and the transition from a 'closed group' with the main focus on substance misuse to a 'mainstream service' youth club. This would offer continuing support and opportunity to maintain contact with a vulnerable group without labelling them. The 'Communities Against Drugs' funding also provided after school provision for those children at a high level of vulnerability. However, due to lack of transport and the belief that a young person should be able to make their own way, this did result in some of the young people losing contact. For those who had continued transport provision, contact with the service has been maintained.

The workers evaluation and the development of themes and messages for practice are detailed in the next section.

Key themes from the group work experience

Throughout the group work process, experiential exercises and techniques gave the young people the opportunity to share their experiences and feelings. This gave the facilitators an insight into the reality of their lives. The internal working models expressed by the young people and the information shared during the discussions were enlightening and often covered themes which the facilitators had not recognised prior to the programme. Many of these themes are discussed in *The Highs and Lows of Family Life* (Kearney et al., 2005).

Differing impact of sibling substance misuse and parental substance misuse

The young people's experiences were often quite different if they were living with sibling misuse as opposed to parental misuse. Parental misuse in some situations led to the failure to carry out basic parenting tasks to meet the physical and emotional needs of the child (see Chapter 1). However, most parents of those attending the group appeared to be taking some steps to 'protect' their child from the worst effects of their substance misuse. This was not the case in relation to sibling misuse. Older siblings were less likely to try and protect their younger siblings from substances, and in fact often spoke openly about it and used substances in front of their younger siblings. This was particularly concerning when this less responsible role is combined with their significant influence on the behaviour and choices of younger family members. In some cases this had led to older siblings sharing substances and teaching their younger sibling about the process of substance misuse.

> *Practice Scenario 2*
>
> Jack, a 12-year-old boy, revealed an in-depth knowledge about injecting into the neck. His older brother had told him how it was done. He had then witnessed his brother injecting substances.

Normalisation of criminal behaviour

The young people showed a general acceptance and awareness of high levels of criminal and risky behaviour, from the use of illicit drugs to witnessing extreme violence and intimidation. Most of the young people were aware of the illegality and the process of procuring drugs. '*Gouching, rattling, and stoned*' were common words used by the children in the group and used in the correct context.

Many lived in neighbourhoods or had extended family members where drug use was the norm.

> *Practice Scenario 3*
>
> An eight year old suggested in the group that, 'My mum takes smack when she has had an argument with her boyfriend and has problems'. Her perception was that you take drugs when you needed to get rid of your problems.

Many young people had witnessed violent attacks on their family as a direct result of substance misuse. High levels of violence were tolerated as the norm, with young people talking, without emotion, of attacks and threats. This was a group of children and young people who were living under the constant shadow of violence. The illegality of their family's behaviour had for some led to experiences of police raids on their homes, parental arrest, and, on occasion, imprisonment.

Stigma

Most participants had experienced abuse, such as being taunted at school or shouted at in the street. The shame and stigma expressed by many of the young people was severe. Many participants lived in properties which had been damaged either by angry neighbours or by those involved in the illicit drug market.

Learning from their experiences

Through this work, listening to the children's experiences and how they made sense of what was happening in their lives, it became apparent that they did not always relate their parents or sibling's behaviour to the effect of substance misuse, but often internalised this as a reflection on the relationship the substance misuser had with them.

Some of the young people were already beginning to minimise the risks apparent in their own behaviour, making this group extremely vulnerable to accidents, substance misuse and potential abuse.

False and broken promises

Many of the young people spoke about being let down by their parents. For the young people this was not the broader concept of unpredictable parenting as identified by the practitioners, but more specific to everyday occurrences. This was often that simple promises and arrangements (including trips out, birthday presents, or what would be for tea) were never carried through. In other words *'Being promised to go to the pictures that doesn't happen'*.

The inconsistency and uncertainty of parental behaviour and responses was particularly significant for those children living away from home. The broken promises often related to parents non-attendance at contact. This caused sadness, disappointment and anger for the young people involved. This left a regular sense of disappointment for some of the young people, and more concerning, a developing expectation that they would always be let down by others. This perception was impinging on their ability to form positive relationships.

The impact of treatment and relapse

Most of the young people had experience of their parents and sibling's attempts to change their substance misusing behaviour. Practitioners traditionally see these attempts at change as a positive step for the well being of all family members. Our young people voiced contradictory opinions. For many the pre-change family life was seen as preferable to the unpredictability of attempts at behaviour change and the almost inevitable relapse which change entails. Young people had experienced a range of emotions when trying to cope with parental change and the facilitators likened this to a roller coaster of change for those young people involved. Addressing a dependency can be an extremely difficult process, and Prochaska and DiClemente's (1982) *Cycle of Change* is an excellent tool in charting change progress. However, this model does not account for the emotions that the child experiences as a parent moves through each difficult stage. Young people described feelings of guilt and blame if their parents were struggling with change: 'It's because I'm naughty', and often described the need to be extra vigilant once the process of change had begun, taking responsibility themselves for what was happening in the household:

Dad's been in bed all day, he's whizzing again.

Mum's not tidied up today, she's been sleeping on the couch all day, Dad shouted at me because my bedroom was a mess.

Poverty

The majority of the children who attended the groups were living in poverty. Most of those living with parental substance misuse had experienced the family's income being spent on drugs. For most, basic needs were met but there was little money left for small treats, school activities or more expensive toys.

Theft within families was a common experience for the young people and unpredictable finances were a part of every day life:

> *She's always demanding money, she has stolen my advantage Game Boy, and my new clothes for my holiday.*

Even for those children now living with grandparents, finances were often strained. Many were living with their grandparents on a voluntary basis, with no formal statutory arrangement, exempting the family from regular financial support from social services (Farmer, 2006). Many extended family carers would not claim child benefit for fear that this would cause arguments within the family. This often left them managing financially only on basic benefits or a pension.

Messages for practice

This group work has informed practice in our area by offering key messages for practitioners working in this field. The evaluation of the group supports ACDM's *Hidden Harm* (2003):

> *Work is required to develop means of enabling the children of problem drug users safely to express their thoughts and feelings about their circumstances.*

However, we are very concerned that the government has rejected the recommendation, in the same document, for longitudinal studies into the impact of familial substance misuse on children (DfES, 2005a).

Roller coaster of change

It was evident that as drug using parents start treatment and enter the *Cycle of Change*, children go round the cycle with them. Signs of maintenance and relapse show through comments made by the young people. The young people did not always know and link these signs to drug use, treatment or relapse, but commented on the changes and differences in appearances, behaviours and actions that affected them.

Picking up on these signs of change and consequent inconsistencies in parenting can only be described as a *Roller Coaster of Change*. As they go round the cycle the more excluded from social activities the children become (Fiona Harbin will consider this in more detail in Chapter 6).

Risk

The children's level of knowledge and understanding of substance misuse was considerable. The child's awareness of the level of risk they perceived themselves to be in, was very different to the level of risk we saw them in. Because criminal behaviour is normalised and accepted, their perceived levels of risk and fear is lower than ours. This reduced perception of risk could lead them into early involvement in criminal and substance activity.

Assertive and proactive outreach

Assertive outreach is needed to engage these hard to reach children and young people. Being proactive in the engagement process with young people is essential. Because of chaotic and unsettled lifestyles, the children attending the group had to be resourceful around the whereabouts of their carers. This could only be done with flexible staff that took the time to find their carers or be bothered to find the young people when they didn't appear at the pick up point. Picking children up straight from school seemed to be most effective method of ensuring group attendance.

Flexible transport

A crucial part in engaging these hard to reach young people is social activity. We tried various ways of picking the children up for the groups, using community transport, taxis and staff from the group. The best way of engaging these young people involved the staff from the groups picking them straight up from school, jointly working with the schools to prepare the young person and remind the parents of the pick up. Picking the children up straight from school excludes the factors that prevent them from attending the group. It also enabled a flexible way of working with families that tend to move around a lot.

Endings and exit strategies

Endings and exit strategies are crucial in running this type of group. Exit strategies should be considered and explained before the group begins and should be included in early discussions with children and carers. The following points seemed the most important:

- Agree on the nature of the group – closed or open.
- Arrange suitable mainstream service provider to maintain social inclusion and contact for each other and monitor level of vulnerability.
- Make links between closed group and mainstream service provider, to look at link worker to keep in touch.
- Agreed referral point if there are any concerns and who to involve.
- Ongoing support to be arranged for the most vulnerable in the group.

- Call back sessions.
- Possible longitudinal study of young people who took part.
- Funding to be secured to maintain provision and transport.
- A take home pack of useful numbers and how to contact the workers if needed.

Adolescence and adulthood – intervening around transition

The government acknowledges that supporting transitions is one of the six key areas of knowledge and skill in child care (DfES, 2005b). This transition stage is of particular importance for children affected by familial substance misuse. Many children and young people have experienced the impact of substance misuse either from siblings, parents or a close family member. The message coming from research is that this group of young people are at risk of substance misuse themselves, the threat of being looked after, the early involvement in criminal activity and are at risk of exploitation and abuse. The Health Advisory Service 1996 has developed four tiers of delivering drug education, advice and treatment services to young people that suggests tier one and two interventions would meet their need. This vulnerable group need specific therapeutic interventions. The group work approach can be very beneficial in meeting their needs and in helping them through a particularly difficult transition period (see Chapter 8).

Running the groups has led to one particular insight into young people's lives, that is that we need to offer early intervention to this particularly vulnerable group who are at risk of early engagement in substance misuse activity.

Conclusion

This chapter does not seek to claim that group work is the 'answer' to all the needs of children and young people brought up in substance misusing families. But what it does do is to suggest that group work is an effective part of the whole 'toolkit' for meeting these needs.

As the recognition of the impact of substance use on this vulnerable group of young people grows, the government and local agencies are committed to develop services to better meet their needs. *Hidden Harm* (ACMD, 2003) recommends:

> . . . *the voices of the children of problem drug users should be heard and listened to.*

and that:

> . . . *work is required to develop means of enabling the children of problem drug users safely to express the thoughts and feeling about their circumstances.*

For many years the needs of this specific group have not been addressed or supported by funding bodies. It has fallen to an enthusiastic few to offer support and intervention at an early stage. If local authorities take these messages on board it may help to better develop service provision specifically tailored to meet the needs of these children who are experiencing the effects of parental and sibling drug and alcohol misuse.

References

ACDM (2003) *Hidden Harm*. London: Home Office.

DfES (2005a) *Government Response to Hidden Harm*. London: HMSO.

DfES (2005b) *Common Core of Skills and Knowledge for the Children's Workforce*. London: HMSO.

Dwidevi, K.N.(1993) *Groupwork with Children and Adolescents*. London: Jessica Kingsley.

Farmer, R. (2006) *Kinship and Unrelated Foster Care Compared: Placement Patterns and Outcomes*. Bristol: University of Bristol Press.

Gilligan, R. (2001) *Promoting Resilience*. London: BAAF.

Harbin, F. (2000) Therapeutic Work with Children of Substance Misusing Parents. In Harbin, F. and Murphy, M. *Substance Misuse and Child Care: How to Understand, Assist and Intervene when Drugs Affect Parenting*. Lyme Regis: Russell House Publishing.

Harbin, F. and Murphy, M. (2003) The Assessment of Parental Substance Misuse and its Impact on Child Care. In Calder, M. and Hackett, S. *Assessment in Child Care*. Lyme Regis: Russell House Publishing.

Hoffman, J. and Su, S.S. (1998) Parental Substance use Disorder, Mediating Variables and Adolescent Drug Use: A Non-recursive Model. *Addiction*. 93: 1135–64.

Jones, L. and O'Loughlin, T. (2003) *A Child Concern Model to Embrace the Framework*. In Calder, M. and Hackett, S. *Assessment in Child Care*. Lyme Regis: Russell House Publishing.

Kearney, J. and Taylor, N. (2001) *The Highs and Lows of Family Life*. Salford: University of Salford.

Kearney, J., Harbin, F., Murphy, M., Wheeler, E. and Whittle, J. (2005) *The Highs and Lows of Family Life: Familial Substance Misuse from a Child's Perspective*. Bolton: Bolton ACPC.

Prochaska, J. and DiClemente, C. (1982) *Transtheoretical Therapy: Towards a More Integrative Model of Change*. Homewood Ill.: Dow Jones/Irwin.

Velleman, R. and Orford, J. (1999) *Risk and Resilience: Adults who were Children of Problem Drinkers*. Amsterdam: Harwood Academic Press.

Chapter 4

Separation, Substance Misuse and Children in Alternative Care

Deborah Evans and Fiona Harbin

Work is required to develop means of enabling the children of problem drug users safely to express their thoughts and feelings about their circumstances.

(ACMD, 2003)

Introduction

It is estimated that between 200,000 and 300,000 children and young people in the UK have parents with serious drug problems. Of these five per cent are in the looked after system, and many of these are placed with foster carers (ACMD, 2003). A number of children will be placed in alternative living situations, usually with extended family members or friends, whilst a minority may be adopted. Some of these children may have experienced the double adversity of familial domestic violence and substance misuse and may well be living in a refuge (Harwin and Forrester, 2005). The ACMD report found that only 37 per cent of fathers and 64 per cent of mothers studied were still living with their children.

Despite the significance of parental substance misuse within the 'looked after' system, there are still very few services tailored to meet the needs of this group. In spite of some improvements in assessment processes and the development of multi-agency protocols for working with drug using parents, there still appears to be a dearth of supportive interventions specifically for those children who have experienced parental substance misuse.

This chapter will explore the possibilities of offering therapeutic group work interventions for the children of substance misusing parents placed with foster and adoptive carers. Consideration will be given to the appropriateness of this approach and how it can be adapted to meet the needs of individual children and their carers.

The possible impacts of parental substance misuse

Parental substance misuse may have a two-fold effect on children. Firstly, the substance may have a direct effect on their parent's ability to provide appropriate care. Many substances impact detrimentally on the 'critical' parent who foresees danger, offers supervision and guidance, and who provides consistent caring within clear boundaries. A parent's mental and physical health may also be impaired as a result of their substance use (Cleaver et al., 1999). Secondly, the indirect effect of substance misuse on the parents' lifestyle. The child may have witnessed drug use, drug dealing, offending behaviour, threats of, or actual violence, poverty, separation, imprisonment, risky associates, and unsafe neighbourhoods. The social experience of children living in such environments can be severely restricted with friendships and social activities thwarted by the home conditions. Commonly children living in these circumstances take on emotional and practical responsibility in the household for themselves, their parents and often younger siblings (Kearney et al., 2005).

This two-fold effect may impair emotional, social and behavioural development in children. These effects may mirror those experienced by seriously abused children including confusion, shame, guilt, fear, helplessness and isolation. The added element of secrecy that exists in many substance-misusing families places the child in an emotional quandary. Children are often reluctant to talk about their home environment for fear of being taken from their parents, parental imprisonment or reprisals from the family. However, not telling leaves the child alone, attempting to live in an environment that fails to consistently meet their basic needs. It is often only when living in a safe alternative environment that children begin to share some of their experiences and the reality of their day-to-day life. It is important to take this opportunity to offer appropriate therapeutic involvement for the child or young person.

Children living away from home due to parental substance misuse may have experienced concerning levels of neglect and emotional abuse (Harwin and Forrester, 2005). Some research (Kelley et al., 1991; Kolar et al., 1994) suggests that for the newly born and young infant the direct effect on the developing brain may be long lasting and irreversible. In later years the cumulative effects on a child's sense of identity, self-esteem and feelings of worth are adversely affected. Research (Alison, 2000) consistently highlights significant social, emotional, intellectual and physical differences between children exposed to early adversity and control groups. The long-term needs of this group of children are therefore complicated and not easily resolved by removal from their adverse living environment.

The child's experience of parent figures may well have informed them that adults:

- Are inconsistent in their response.
- Are emotionally unavailable for long periods whilst under the influence of substances.
- Fail to maintain adequate physical care and safety in the home.

- Cannot be trusted to place the child's needs before their own.
- Cannot be trusted to respect the child's personal belongings.

This 'internal working model' (Howe et al., 1999) of the world may have left children with adapted behaviours developed as coping strategies to aid survival. Some of these strategies will be no longer appropriate when living with caring adults who are committed to consistently meeting the child's basic needs. However, it may be some time before the child feels able to trust the caregiver sufficiently to consider relinquishing those strategies. Alternative carers need guidance in understanding how difficult it is for a child who has been let down by parent figures to trust another adult in a parenting role. Carers need to emphasise the positive aspects of parenting by taking responsibility as an adult, initiating attachment and creating a secure base from which the developing child can grow (SCIE, 2004). By consistently meeting the needs of their child and placing those needs as a priority within the family setting, carers will encourage trust to develop, thus aiding resolution of any distorted survival strategies. A parent figure who provides 'unconditional positive regard' (Rogers, 1961) to a child helps to boost the child's self-esteem and feelings of self-worth. In consistently highlighting the child's strengths and promoting opportunities for enjoyment and achievement, the carer boosts the resilience of the child. Aided by such positive intervention the child can feel confident in their ability to succeed and develop coping strategies and personal strengths that will be beneficial. That carers can affect the child's ability to find some resolution should not be underestimated. 'Both personal inborn characteristics and the social context interact to promote or diminish resilience' (Clarke and Clarke, 2001).

Children placed in alternative care will be coping with issues of separation and loss. Those who have experienced significant levels of parental substance misuse may have experienced levels of neglect and emotional abuse. The cumulative effects on their sense of identity, self-esteem and feelings of worth can be complicated. These problems are often exacerbated by the child's fear for their own future health or behaviour. Research here from Gilligan (2001) show carers need to be careful not to compound these difficulties by inadvertently reinforcing ideas that the child may have been damaged because of maternal substance misuse or will develop future problems of addiction and dependency. This sense of hopelessness can hinder supportive interventions. Children and young people need reassurance that with the right support and care they are able to lead healthy and fulfilling lives. Parenting in alternative families should reinforce that the child is valued, loved and can rely on the adults to unconditionally meet their needs.

Skills for working with children and young people

Many practitioners may experience anxiety or lack of confidence when working with children who have experienced trauma. We may worry about making the young person feel worse by encouraging them to talk about their experiences. We may not feel confident to deal with the young person's distress or worry about igniting a fresh disclosure. The issues of clarity, confidentiality and feedback all serve to inhibit attempts to initiate a meaningful exchange between worker and child. Structural issues such as workloads, availability of appropriate spaces and the provision of good supervision may also block workers' attempts to work directly with children and young people.

All of these inhibiting factors are exacerbated when working with children who have lived with substance misuse. The additional factors we may experience include concerns about what to say to the child, what language to use and our own level of knowledge regarding substances (perhaps the child will know more than the worker!). How should we approach the subject of safety planning and how do we manage issues of identity? Practitioners may have fears for their own safety because of the 'risky' adults linked to the child's family. How does the practitioner help the child cope with these violent and intimidating adults and will doing the work mean that they are at risk?

We believe many practitioners already possess the skills required to help the child resolve their past experiences and aid their future development. Direct work skills include:

- Listening to the child.
- Conveying genuine interest.
- Empathetic concern.
- Understanding.
- Emotional warmth.
- Respect for the child.
- Capacity to manage and contain the assessment.
- Awareness of the entire transaction between worker and child.
- Self-management.
- Technique.

(Jones, 2003)

These skills reflect Rogers' (1961) core conditions, required to produce a sufficient therapeutic environment. They are linked to the common core skills for all practitioners required to fully meet the needs of children and young people (DfES, 2005).

Wheeler (Ch. 3) describes a basis for good communication as:

- Being genuine and sincere.
- Being interested.
- Being yourself within your professional framework.
- Accepting you are not the expert.
- Letting the young person be your teacher.
- Accept you will make mistakes but be easy on yourself.
- Consult with others.

Aims and objectives of direct work

We need to have a range of interventions at our disposal. These may include simple low key interventions aimed at validating the child's experience and affirming their right to have their needs met, through to more complex, longer-term therapy. All interventions should be aimed at helping the child recover from their experiences and subsequently moving on to a healthier future.

The level of intervention may be based on the skills, role and objectives of the worker and the readiness of the child or young person to engage in the therapeutic process. The agreement set out at the start of the work should depict the purpose of the work and the areas to be covered. The therapeutic goals of any intervention should be to establish a relationship that allows the child to:

- Reflect on their experiences.
- Express their feelings about those experiences.
- Release pent up emotions in appropriate ways within a safe environment.
- Resolve powerful feelings of loss and confusion.
- Develop age appropriate behaviours and dependency on adult figures.
- Explore age appropriate risk taking to challenge any distorted ideologies.

The appropriateness of group work

For a general discussion of the appropriateness of groupwork as an intervention, please see Chapter 3.

Our experience of working with the children of substance misusers revealed that it was not only birth parents but also foster carers and extended family members who were reluctant for children to attend a specific group. Parents, perhaps unsurprisingly, recognised that a group would entail their child revealing some information about their home life and more specifically their parent's substance misuse. This provoked a fear that their children might be taken into care. Foster carers and extended family members expressed different reservations. These included concerns that group attendance might unsettle a currently stable placement, that the child may be given too much information on drugs and this may lead to them experimenting with substances, and that association with other children with experience of parental substance misuse would be detrimental to future stability. Carers often saw their placement as a new safer world, away from drug use and the criminal and dangerous activities that go with it. Through association at the group, carers feared that their 'drug-free' idyll might be broken.

Group work is not always the most appropriate intervention at any given time. Many children who have experienced parental substance misuse may not wish to attend a group. Some children may not feel comfortable in a group setting, some may prefer individual supportive interventions, and some young people may not want to attend for reasons of confidentiality, especially if they now feel safe and settled in placement.

Adopted children may perceive such a group as a retrograde step, strengthening their links with a birth family they have left behind and jeopardising their identity as part of their new adoptive family.

Aims and objectives

A range of interventions may be considered within the group, from low key interventions to validate the child's experience and affirm their right to have their needs met, through to more complex longer-term therapy. All interventions should be aimed at helping the child recover from their experiences, including the loss of parent figures and subsequent moving on. The level of intervention may be based on the skills of the workers facilitating the group, or on a set of agreed aims and objectives at a more strategic level. Whatever the impetus, once the therapeutic goals have been established and set out as clear aims and objectives for the group, consideration can then be given to how these may be met.

Planning the group

There are many factors to consider at the planning stage, not only regarding the therapeutic input but also the demography and practicalities of the group process:

- *Size:* The size of the group should allow for full participation of all the group members. Depending on the ages of the children and the number of facilitators, 8–10 members should be an ideal at the outset. Allowing for the dropout of some of the children, the group would possibly drop to 6–7 members.
- *Compatibility:* It is important to take every step to make the group compatible, taking into account the age, gender, developmental stage, cultural background, race, and ethnicity of the children, as well as their life experiences. Our experience showed that the more compatible the group the more beneficial it appeared to be.
- *Therapeutic interventions:* This decision has to be the choice of those who are running the group. Sessions drawing on direct work skills alongside skills such as brief therapy, family therapy methods, counselling, educative resources, non-directive interviewing and the knowledge of attachment, would provide more than enough material to meet the group's aims and objectives.
- *Timescale:* The group may run as an ongoing open ended support group (in which case it is likely that sessions would be semi-structured with some overlap to incorporate new members) or as a more structured time limited programme. For the purposes of this chapter we have considered a programme of structured sessions over a 6–8 week period. However, the programme and the ideas for sessions could be easily transferable to a semi-structured drop-in group or individual work with a child.
- *Open or closed?* Whether the group is open or closed is likely to depend on whether it is time limited or ongoing. Ideally if the group is time limited and following a

structured programme of sessions it should be closed, allowing the participants to work through sensitive issues with a familiar group of children. An ongoing support group should be able to accommodate new members and therefore this could be an open group.

- *Facilitators:* This is likely to be governed by organisational and structural constraints. Managerial support is essential as the commitment cannot be underestimated. Group work can be complex and demanding; two workers to plan and run the group are essential with three workers being desirable. Our own experience has indicated that half a working day per week is required to plan the group, facilitate, debrief, and complete recording.
- *Recording:* Arrangements for recording will depend on the protocol and policy of the lead agency. However, this needs to be agreed at the outset and clearly explained to the young people, the carers and key workers, to avoid confusion at a later stage.
- *Support for carers:* Support for the carers of the children attending the group should be made available. The group will inevitably raise issues which may impact on their behaviour or emotional well being at home. The Adoption and Children Act 2000 places a duty on local authorities to provide support to adopters, their children and birth families. This work should pay particular attention to the specific needs of newly formed families and aim to promote attachments and secure a life long family for the child.
- *Confidentiality:* This needs to be clearly agreed at the outset and a written policy needs to be available for the participants, the carers, the parents, and the referring agency. Any information regarding child protection concerns cannot be confidential but everyone needs to be clear how other discussions in the group will be recorded and who will have access to this material. Very young children can understand the concept of sharing and these should be considered in written or verbal form depending on the age range in the group.
- *Evaluation:* It is likely that your groups, like ours, will develop over time. Most of the development of our groups has come from evaluation. With reference to the aims and objectives, by the use of interviews, questionnaires and group games the views of the participants, the facilitators, the carers, and the referring agency have contributed to a thorough evaluation of each group work programme and hopefully, an improvement in the facilitation of the next group.
- *Government and local strategy:* The government's updated Drug Strategy (2002), identifies children whose parents misuse substances, and young people in the looked after system as vulnerable, suggesting that they are in need of extra support. Every local authority should have its own Young People's Substance Misuse Strategy, which should identify resources, education plans and staff training around young people and substance misuse. It is important that any group run for this group of young people fits into the local strategy.
- *Establishing a contract:* Facilitators may use contracts to outline objectives, expectations and issues of confidentiality. This may be particularly relevant for older

age groups but can be equally effective with younger children and are especially useful to set out boundaries and expectations regarding behaviour. A contract with the child or young person could include times and venue, what you will cover in each session (with ideas generated from the child), what activities you may wish to include, what the child can expect from the worker and what the worker expects from the child. It is especially important that levels of confidentiality and feedback are agreed and stated in the contract. It is important that children are re-assured that information will not be passed to aggressive adults unless it is done in a manner that ensures their safety. Current carers should understand this and if part of the extended family network must ensure that information is not passed on. Contracts with parent figures should include an over-view of the work to be achieved and the likely impact on the child. It could also outline any expectations of the carers whilst the work is undertaken. Parent figures may benefit from guidance on how to manage any behaviours resulting from the work.

Establishing the work plan

Facilitators need to arrange an appropriate venue, taking into consideration the age of participants, the type of activities to be used, the time of year and what equipment is required. The programme of work should include a variety of both individual and group exercises, allowing for some energetic work and some quieter periods. Role-play, video, artwork and sculpting can help engage preferred styles of group members. Facilitators should have a good understanding of group work principles expecting the different stages of the group work process (norming, forming, storming, performing and ending). A good understanding of the impact that adversity can have on children is vital, as is some assessment of the children, including their past experiences and attachment behaviours.

Facilitators should use the assessment to plan when feelings work should be introduced. Ideally, life story work should have been completed with each child before group work starts. The aim of the group is to help resolve any substance misuse issues and will not have time to undertake life story work (although there may be some cross-over at times).

Ideas for a work plan

This section considers the typical aims for each session and how these may be achieved. Types of activities are included but the specific details of these have been left open for the facilitators to decide, using their own skills and imagination.

Seven sessions have been outlined, but many topics cannot be fully covered in one session, and may spread over a period of weekly activities.

Session 1

This first session should include exercises to introduce participants to each other and the group work programme. If contracts are being used they should be addressed early and in an age appropriate way. Participants can decide on group rules and these can be incorporated into the contract. Issues of confidentiality should be discussed in this session even when they have been discussed during the home visits when planning the group. The rest of the session should be taken up with forming activities.

Session 2

The second session should include more forming activities, including some that allow for the sharing of personal details. Depending on the age of participants this may be achieved verbally or through artwork. All the activities should be safe, quick and good fun. There should be an expectation that the children only need share a little information about themselves. Helping children and young people to introduce their world may take up all of this session. By the end of the session facilitators should have information regarding who is significant to the child, who the child has lived with both now and in the past and some basic information about those significant relationships. The facilitators should be clear that they value all types of family composition, normalising experiences as much as possible, and especially reinforcing that many children live away from their family of origin and it is not their fault.

Session 3

At some point early in the life of the group it is important that there is some work on substances and their impact. The children will be aware of their parents' substance misuse and may have made sense of this in ways informed by misconception and fear. This group of children and young people need clear and sensible advice on the effects of substances. There are now many publications and websites available to guide staff on drug education. As a starting point quizzes and card games can work well with older children. For younger children a general discussion around things that are good and bad for the body, can lead to information sharing and questions. Drug misuse can be explained to younger children in a holistic way by facilitating discussion on the impact of all substances on the body. Using body templates and doing this pictorially can be a helpful introduction. Examining the difference between prescribed drugs that help make us better and those that do the body harm is a simple concept which most younger children will understand. Our experience has been that even young children have heard of heroin and cocaine, but do not understand what they really are.

It is important to introduce the concept of risk as it relates to substances, and for older children, who may disclose their own substance use, there may be a need for harm reduction education at a basic level. We have successfully introduced harm reduction by the use of 'what next' scenarios and role-play, where, through depersonalised discussion, children and young people have explored the consequences of risky behaviour, and come up with their own safety strategies.

Session 4

By this session the group may know each other reasonably well and feel safe to share more personal information. If possible, it is important to give everyone the opportunity to tell their story. Activities to aid this should be age appropriate. We have found artwork is very useful for all ages, but more energetic young people have chosen to re-tell their story using drama. The facilitators need to give positive messages about coping skills as each story is told. Affirming exercises should be used to reinforce the resilience and worthiness of participants. If stories have highlighted the unmet needs of the participants, the facilitators should help participants to identify how their needs are being met now. Alternatively exercises to enhance a sense of identity, aiding positive links to parent figures, whilst accepting that the parents had difficulties meeting their needs. Children need to feel that they can be 'like' their parent, without the negative connotation, so positive factors should be explored.

Session 5

Participants will now have indicated their willingness or resistance to exploring their past or current relationships. Exercises to allow this to happen should be planned. Questionnaires, artwork, and making videos can be useful in exploring different emotions. By this stage of the group participants may be sharing more information about their relationships at home and their experiences of substance misuse. It is important that at each stage the facilitators challenge distorted thinking sensitively and develop notions of safety and adult responsibility.

Our experiences have shown that use of drama and role-play can be very helpful as a tool that facilitates the sharing of information and experiences. Children can participate in safety, in a non-personal manner. For those who do not wish to participate on an acting basis, allowing the children to stage-manage a role-play with all the behind the scenes tasks can work well.

Session 6

As the group becomes more established and confident in each other's company, further work on feelings can be explored. Exercises about what makes people happy and sad, practicing expressing positive and negative emotions, and looking at ways of coping with strong feelings, are all helpful for the young people. Specific consideration should be given to coping with loss, as all the young people have lost their birth family through living in a foster or adoptive placement. Many of the young people will have experienced the death of a parent or family member. In our experience, the majority had experienced the premature death or serious illness of a close family member due to substance misuse. The young people were familiar with their parent's symptoms of withdrawal and overdose, although they may not have known the cause of the symptoms.

Session 7

This final session is important in building strengths for the future. The young people need to have identified significant people whom they can turn to for support. Young people have indicated that they like to put this information, either written or pictorially in a workbook, which they can take away with them. It is important to empower the child, to give them confidence and skills, which they can take away. The use of basic safety training proved popular in achieving this aim. Enabling the young people to practice asking for help, role playing calls to the emergency services, and teaching very basic first aid skills, gave the young people some practical skills that they could use in the future.

This final session should include time for the young people to identify strengths and positive messages for their future with alternative families.

Exit strategies

The group work programme may raise issues for the child which may need addressing outside the group. It is important that there is appropriate support for the young person during, and on completion of, the group work programme. The following can provide a basis for an ongoing support package for the young people who have completed the group work programme and their carers:

- Ongoing individual support for the young person.
- Ongoing individual support for the carers.
- Ongoing membership at local groups for young people to encourage socialisation and prevent isolation.
- Consultation and support at times of crisis for the whole family.
- Call back session for the group.
- Facilitating young people telling other young people about the group through the development of a booklet or leaflet, exhibitions, or videoing.
- Follow up session, to involve young people and their carers, to promote the young people maintaining links with each other outside the group environment.

Conclusion

There is widespread evidence that parental substance misuse is increasingly impacting on children and young people living in alternative care. There are existing systems which offer support to children in care, and living with adoptive families. These systems work well and support should now be available for young people and their carers. However, many children and young people who have lived with parental substance misuse have specific therapeutic needs and there are often many similarities in their experiences. To address these themes a group work approach can be beneficial.

For many years the specific needs of this group of young people have not been addressed. As the recognition of the impact of parental drug use increases, practitioners and managers may need to develop services to meet the need. Many different intervention programmes are being offered throughout the country, sometimes these are a result of the enthusiasm of individual practitioners rather than a strategic decision. However, the future could be positive for the development of more specific services. *Hidden Harm* (ACMD, 2003) recommends: '. . . the voices of the children of problem drug users should be heard and listened to' and that '. . . work is required to develop means of enabling the children of problem drug users safely to express their thoughts and feelings about their circumstances'.

If this is taken on board by local authorities and Children's Trusts it can only be positive for those children and young people who have and are experiencing parental substance misuse, and may lead to development of more service provision specifically tailored to their needs.

References

ACMD (2003) *Hidden Harm*. London: Advisory Council on the Misuse on Drugs.

Alison, L. (2000) What are the Risks to Children of Parental Substance Misuse? In Harbin, F. and Murphy, M. (2000) *Substance Misuse and Child Care: How to Understand, Assist and Intervene when Drugs Affect Parenting*. 9–20. Lyme Regis: Russell House Publishing.

Clarke, A. and Clarke, A. (2001) Early Adversity and Adoptive Solutions. *Adoption and Fostering*, 25: 1.

Cleaver, H., Unell, I. and Aldgate, J. (1999) *Children's Needs: Parenting Capacity*. London: HMSO.

DfES (2005) *Common Core of Skills and Knowledge for the Children's Workforce*. London: HMSO.

Gilligan, R. (2001) *Promoting Resilience: A Resource Guide on Working with Children in the Care System*. London: BAAF.

Harbin, F. (2000) Therapeutic Work with Children of Substance Misusing Parents. In Harbin, F. and Murphy, M. (2000) *Substance Misuse and Child Care*. Lyme Regis: Russell House Publishing.

Harwin, J. and Forrester, D. (2005) *Parental Substance Misuse and Child Welfare*. London: Nuffield.

Howe, D., Brandon, M., Hinnings, D. and Schofield, G. (1999) *Attachment Theory, Child Maltreatment and Family Support: A Practice and Assessment Guide*. Basingstoke: Palgrave/MacMillan.

Jones, P.H. (2003) *Communicating with Vulnerable Children*. London: Gaskell/DoH.

Kearney, J., Harbin, F., Murphy, M., Wheeler, E. and Whittle, J. (2005) *The Highs and Lows of Family Life: Familial Substance Misuse from a Child's Perspective*. Bolton: Bolton ACPC.

Kelley, S.J., Walsh, J.H. and Thompson, K. (1991) Birth Outcomes, Health Problems and Neglect with Prenatal Exposure to Cocaine. *Pediatric Nursing*. 17: 130–6.

Kolar, A. et al. (1994) Children of Substance Abusers: The Life Experiences of Children of Opiate Addicts in Methadone Maintenance. *American Journal of Drug and Alcohol Abuse.* 20: 159–71.

Murphy, M. and Harbin, F. (2003) The Assessment of Parental Substance Misuse and its Impact on Child Care. In Calder, M.C. *Assessment in Child Care: Using and Developing Frameworks for Practice.* Lyme Regis: Russell House Publishing.

Rogers, C. (1961) *On Becoming a Person.* Boston: Houghton Mifflin.

Chapter 5

Children, Alcohol and Family Violence

Deborah Evans

Introduction

Much has been written about the adverse impact of being parented within the context of domestic violence. Hester et al. (2000) define domestic violence as any violent or abusive behaviour which is used by one person to control and dominate another with whom they have or have had a relationship. Mullender and Humphries (1998), Cleaver et al. (1999) and others succinctly highlight the significant immediate and long-term effects that living with domestic violence can have on the lives of children. Similar research concerns the ways in which parental substance misuse can affect the lives and general well being of children (Kearney et al., 2005). There are some research studies informing us of the detrimental effects for children of living with parent figures who are reliant on alcohol (Velleman, 1993; Laybourn et al., 1996; Houston et al., 1997; Harwin and Forrester, 2005), although these are fewer than in regard to domestic violence or substance misuse. Whilst all these areas of research are of interest to child care practitioners there is little literature on the complexity of dual or triple concern. Practitioners know that in their day-to-day work with families the issues of domestic violence, alcohol and or substance misuse are often simultaneously found. The use of substances, particularly alcohol, may act as a disinhibitor, a catalyst or a precursor to violence. Illegal or prescription drugs and alcohol may be used by victims of domestic violence as a coping strategy complicating the effects of living with a violent and controlling partner. Women who live with domestic violence are more likely to misuse prescription drugs as well as alcohol (Stark and Flitcraft, 1998). Women who abuse substances are generally more vulnerable to all kinds of abuse including domestic violence. Around a third of incidents of domestic violence are linked to alcohol misuse. Over time these inappropriate adult behaviours have an adverse effect on home conditions and lifestyle, leading to practical environmental difficulties which heighten the negative experience of the child (Cleaver et al., 1999). The effects of domestic violence and the misuse of substances including alcohol, can adversely affect attachment and parenting. When experienced together, alcohol or substance misuse and domestic violence can doubly impact on a child's well being, creating a complex cycle of adult need that disadvantages the vulnerable child.

We need to acknowledge the complexity of assessing families where both adults are violent to each other, and acknowledge that these are different issues to domestic violence (although there may be issues of intimidation and control present). In such circumstances the author advocates a good understanding of the history of violence and perceptions of both adults alongside an assessment of the individual's ability to provide adequate care for any child. Families where violence is the norm and adults are misusing alcohol and or drugs require more than a simplistic assessment of perpetrator and victim advocated by some domestic violence authors. This chapter will explore the links between substances and domestic violence and most importantly explore the child's experience of their interaction. Throughout the chapter case scenarios will be used to highlight the child's view of adult behaviour. All scenarios used are extracts from work undertaken with children and young people.

Adult behaviours and service provision – domestic violence

There has been a growing awareness of the need for government to take a lead in developing services to those families where domestic violence is the norm. Every week two women are killed in England and Wales by their current or former partners and domestic violence accounts for a quarter of all violent crime (Rowsell, 2001). Separation affords limited protection from abuse indeed the act of leaving may provoke an escalation of violence, with women becoming more susceptible to murder by a partner in the post-separation months (Crawford and Garner, 1991 and McNeil, 1987). Successive governments have been slow to put domestic violence on the political agenda, leaving the women's movement and voluntary organisations to take the lead in raising the issue. Recently we have seen government-led initiatives highlighting the need to provide help and support to adults, mainly women living with the threat of violence from a partner. The opening of the first men's refuge in this country in 2004 has helped raise awareness of male abuse and will hopefully provide useful information regarding the problems faced by men abused by their partners. However the link between parenting and domestic violence will remain a serious dilemma primarily for women, as it is women who are overwhelmingly afforded responsibility for child rearing and domestic violence consists predominantly of male to female violence (Abrahams, 1994). When women are violent towards men, the violence is often used as a means of self-defence or reaction to long-term abuse (Dobash and Dobash, 1992).

Many women and children are blocked from seeking outside help by the taboo of admitting there is domestic violence in the home. Women fear they will be blamed for provoking the abuse, criticised for not leaving, be held responsible for the safety of their children and ultimately may lose their children if they disclose (Calder et al., 2004). Statistics suggest women will be assaulted 35 times before they seek help

(Yearnshire, 1997) but that when they do it is often something their children have said or experienced that instigates disclosure. Children and young people are similarly blocked in seeking appropriate help (Hester et al., 2000; Calder, 2005). Up to one third of young people who have experienced domestic violence have never told anyone (Cleaver et al., 1999). This secrecy serves to isolate women and children from appropriate support. Reder and Duncan (1999) found domestic violence was a recurring theme in cases where children had died from maltreatment, showing the importance of understanding the links between violence towards adults and potential fatal maltreatment of children. Farmer and Owen (1995) identified domestic violence as a common thread in families where child abuse concerns had been noted. A failure to link child protection plan recommendations with specific services aimed at reducing the level of violence in the family were noted in at least one study (Stark and Flitcraft, 1995). We know from many reports about child death (Maria Colwell 1974; Kimberley Carlile 1987; Toni Dales 1993; Sukina Hammond, 1994 and others) that for some children this oversight has had tragic consequences. Whilst efforts are made to engage with women as survivors of domestic violence little government funding or policy is aimed at repairing potential damage to the relationship between mother and child. The NCH study (Abrahams, 1994) talked to women in refuges about their children; these women reported that the violence they had endured did have an adverse effect on their parenting. This created an emotional distance between them and their child and a loss of confidence in their ability to effectively parent their children. Women living with domestic violence described being inconsistent in their parenting style, feeling stressed by their child care responsibilities with their standards of care fluctuating depending on the abuse experienced and for some behaving in a punitive manner to their children (Holden and Ritchie, 1991; Brandon and Lewis, 1996). Yet efforts to re-establish a positive parent child bond is often left to refuge staff who may not be skilled in working in this area or have the resources to do this work effectively. As a long-term preventative measure this area of work is not given sufficient priority.

Practice Scenario 1

Simon aged eight years had attended group work for children living with domestic violence. Although he had joined in most activities he had remained almost silent for most of the sessions. Towards the end of one session he went to the flip chart standing in the corner of the room on which was written a heading 'the person who scares me is'. Simon wrote his fathers name underneath then got his coat ready to leave. I asked Simon when did his father scare him and he disclosed details of the violence he had observed towards his mother and the displays of anger his father used to threaten and control family members.

Adult behaviours and service provision – alcohol misuse

1.7 million men and 0.6 million women drink at harmful levels with alcohol related deaths increasing per 100,000 from 10.7 in 2001 to 11.6 in 2003. These figures indicate a sizable problem for society. Many of these adults will present to adult services at some point in their lives for support. It is important that practitioners recognise where there are additional needs relating to parenting responsibilities and discuss how those needs might be addressed. One small UK study, with 44 adults in treatment, parenting 88 children, showed the adults were aware of the impact on their children with over half believing the children were affected by their drinking and a quarter considered that their children were showing signs of disturbed behaviour (Thompson and Blennerhassett, 1996). According to NACOA figures 920,000 children are currently living in a home where one or both parents misuse alcohol and post dated figures suggest 6.2 per cent of adults grew up in a family where one or both parents drank excessively (2000). Alcohol Concern (2001) suggests that 0.78–1.3 million children are affected by alcohol misuse in the family. Some studies suggest that children brought up with parental problem drinking but where there is family harmony and no link to violence are no more likely to develop problems than any other children (Velleman and Orford, 1993). However for most, family life may well be over shadowed by alcohol, with individuals adapting to the problems created by the adult's behaviour.

Practice Scenario 2

When talking about the forthcoming weekend, one ten year old said: 'it's not so good at our house because my mum and dad drink, then they get nasty and start fighting, me and my brother just stay upstairs'. It was clear that for her the anticipation of the weekend was over shadowed by the knowledge that the adults charged with her care would not be able to control their behaviours and she would be left scared and anxious.

In one year there were 72,000 hospital admissions with a diagnosis of mental and behavioural disorders due to alcohol including 31,300 admissions for alcohol dependence syndrome (NACOA, 2000). We need to identify how many of these adults are parents and if their children are in need of services in their own right. But this requires an understanding of responsibilities that cross agencies and service criteria boundaries and some means of collating such data. The services available for adults misusing alcohol are already limited with even less services focusing on the needs of parents and children where alcohol is a problem. The important national link between adult alcohol teams and children's services is yet to be successfully established. There are few cohesive links between the adult based alcohol services and child support services with joint protocols less likely to be used with alcohol services than drug services (Kearney et al., 2000; Harwin and Forrester, 2005).

Despite alcohol being known to have adverse effects on behaviour it is cheap, legal and widely available. Government health initiatives are currently attempting to raise the public's awareness of the health dangers of alcohol consumption and recent media articles have raised the significant cost of anti-social behaviour linked directly to what is called the 'binge culture' of our society. Yet no mention is made of the link between alcohol consumption and parenting of children.

The British Crime Survey (2000) indicates a strong link between alcohol and violence. This is particularly emphasised in government policies and police crime prevention strategies. However, the links to family violence and the possible effects on the lives of children are less well advertised. One could presume that society's main concern is to target those who drink outside the home, many of whom identified in the media are young and single with no dependent children. Some of this group who are violent on the streets will not be violent within the family setting. However, a significant group of adults who misuse alcohol and are violent generally will also pose a direct threat to their family. Less publicised are the significant number who will manage to get home before they unleash any violence. There are a number of adults who do not pose a threat to the community, yet will be violent and intimidating to their family members (McMurran, 1999). The risks posed by older drinkers who consume alcohol inside the home, who may be less of a threat to the community, is not addressed with the same vigour. This aggression and compulsive alcohol misuse outside and inside the home are commonly seen as separate problems and dealt with by separate agencies.

Although there has been a long history of the association between alcohol misuse and family violence (Gordon, 1989) it is only recently that statutory child protection agencies have attempted to work alongside adult alcohol services. These initial attempts have not yet established a healthy communication between adult alcohol services and family support services. The abuse of children in multi-problem families focuses attention on the need for an holistic assessment of all family circumstances with specific services aimed at adult behaviours in order to reduce risk to children. However, there is still a long way to go before we see this kind of collaboration between alcohol and children services to effectively safeguard children. The plight of children whose parents are under the influence of alcohol, could be highlighted by the media as is the plight of children left in other high risk situations. Potentially less damaging risk factors are subject to high profile media campaigns with a consequent shift in societal thinking (for example children left without car safety seats or affected by adult smoking). With strong media messages and supportive policies, community acceptance of certain adult behaviours can be altered.

Adult behaviours and service provision – substance misuse

Hidden Harm (ACMD, 2003) estimates that 250–350,000 children have parents who misuse illicit drugs in the United Kingdom. Exact figures are impossible to establish because of the very nature of substance misuse, and the secrecy that surrounds it. Compounding this difficulty is the taboo of disclosing, as a parent, a substance misuse problem. It is likely therefore that any figures available are likely to be an underestimation of the reality.

It is important that workers are able to form co-operative relationships with parent figures allowing for exploration of all aspects of family strengths and vulnerabilities, including problematic adult behaviour. Skills in engaging with service users in a non-judgemental way, encouraging open and honest dialogue is key to effective partnerships where the needs of children are central (Hamer, 2005). Cleaver and Freeman (1995) found parents were reluctant to disclose problem drinking, domestic violence or other adult difficulties fearing a punitive response. For those families caught up in child protection enquiries, anxiety about the potential loss of children would further restrict openness. Whilst adult drug services are better established within the child protection arena than adult alcohol services, practitioners can still feel the complexity of the problem makes potential for change limited. Children may be identified as children in need yet left living with concerning levels of parental substance misuse, with little support specifically aimed at the child's personal and unique experience. Figures taken from Child Protection Registers indicate that a significant number of children on the register are living with parental substance misuse and it is having a detrimental effect on their well being. Yet, Forrester (2000) found that few substance misuse specialists were invited to Child Protection Conferences and of those who were, half did not attend. Even when children are identified as experiencing significant harm as a result of adult substance misuse, outcomes remain relatively poor with few resources aimed at meeting the needs of those children at an individual level.

The development of services to meet the needs of adults who misuse substances has been high on the British government's agenda over the last 10 years. However the Government Drug Strategy has consistently failed to consider the needs of children and young people living with parental alcohol or drug misuse. *Hidden Harm* (ACMD, 2003) has gone some way to address this issue, but has not as yet been reflected fully in government strategies or policies. The government's response to *Hidden Harm* (DfES, 2005) can only be described as disappointing from a child's point of view. Fortunately, this lack of policy has not prevented the development of some excellent services working specifically with families where there is substance misuse. However, developing protocols for multi-disciplinary working lacks consistency from one local authority to the next (Kearney et al., 2000). Because of the growing acknowledgment that substance misuse takes place within the context of family life, there are a number of drug services aimed at users who are parents or are pregnant. Services aimed at children living with substance misusing parents, but who are not users themselves, are rare. This lack of service provision fails to address the current and future difficulties faced by those children.

Practice Scenario 3

Annabelle (8 years) and her brother Tim (5 years) had lived with their parents high levels of substance misuse all their lives. Their day-to-day existence was regulated by the needs of both parents to acquire significant amounts of heroin, cannabis and alcohol. In order to get their daily supply, the children's mother worked as a prostitute. Home conditions were very poor except for the children's bedrooms which were decorated very well, with warm bedding and lots of toys. All provisions had been supplied by paternal grandparents who managed to support the children sufficiently to ensure their physical needs were met and regularly had the children stay over at weekends to check they were alright. In monitoring the home conditions the couple had become increasingly concerned that the children were witnessing high levels of substance misuse and violence in the home from the many visitors. On one occasion a heroin user had died in the property from an over-dose. Although they loved their son very much and knew he did not want to lose his children the couple referred the situation to social services. Several weeks later when supportive interventions had proved ineffective, paternal grandparents offered long-term care to both children with continued contact with parents. Annabelle told me 'I love my mum and don't want to leave her, if I do she might get really poorly and die'. I was not able to gain Annabelle's agreement to a move from her mother's care even though she later said 'I do get scared at night when people are coming and sometime my mum and dad go out and leave us, but if I wasn't there mum would be very sad'. Annabelle remained committed to the care of her mum, whilst Tim openly announced he 'did not want to return home and wanted to stay with his grandparents forever'. Both children were placed with the grandparents who applied for Residence Orders. The co-operation between grandparents, parents and children remained good with regular contact maintained with both parents. The children did extremely well in primary and secondary school, cultivating a number of friends and hobbies. I was dismayed but not surprised to hear some seven years later that Annabelle had at 15 years old, absconded from her grandparent care, left school where she was expected to achieve 'A grades' and was living rough with her mother. There were concerns that Annabelle was being sexually exploited in order to get money for her mother's drug habit and serious concerns for her rapidly deteriorating health and well being. The overwhelming sense of responsibility towards her mother and the continued influence of her mother's needs and lifestyle eventually proved disruptive to Annabelle. I wonder if professionals had remained involved with Annabelle over time allowing her the opportunity to explore her relationship and perception of her mother, the outcome may have been different. Professionals continue to monitor and try to work with Annabelle and her mother.

Children and young people have a right to feel exasperated by problems in their life created by their parents, but practitioners need to help children to understand the complexity of addiction. There can be similar difficulties for children living with domestic violence where children feel exasperated by a mother who stays with a violent partner (especially if that person isn't their father), or a parent who continues to drink heavily despite mounting health problems. Practitioners need to promote discussion of these issues in age appropriate ways that don't reinforce negative stereotypes of parents. Outlining the problem helps break the secret for children and young people, empowers the child by sharing information and helps develop the idea that they can talk about a problem which is held in common by others. The secrecy will not be broken if children believe what they have experienced is too awful to tell, or something they should be ashamed of.

The cross-over: domestic violence, alcohol and substance misuse

The issue of domestic violence is currently afforded a higher profile than ever before in our society. Unfortunately public awareness is confused by the role modelling of acceptable behaviour by our national heroes and others afforded authority in our society. Continuing to accept the abuse of female partners from those in positions of power (including sportsmen and other celebrities) forgoes the opportunity to send a powerful message to our children and young people that abusing a partner is unacceptable. Currently, we see substantial efforts to address the health of the nation including an emphasis on alcohol and substance misuse. Yet there has been no detailed information cascaded to the general public highlighting the effects on children of the links between parental substance misuse, and incidents of domestic violence. The potential impact on parenting is perhaps most widely accepted, by the general public, in regard to the misuse of drugs. However we are a long way from a similar cultural shift in society's acceptance of alcohol consumption. One British crime survey in 2000 showed that 33 per cent of domestic violence incidents involved people who had been drinking. If the cost of policing such behaviour was added to the statistics for alcohol related street crime and addressed within the same context, it might lead to these adults being assessed for their suitability to return home where there are vulnerable women and children present.

Professionals should ensure that they have a child protection plan that clearly identifies how each member of the core group will address the risk factors including domestic violence, alcohol or substance misuse. Similarly, children in need action plans should address the risks posed by substance misuse by linking adults with appropriate agencies, setting clear targets for change and closely monitoring progress. Protocols for all meetings regarding the needs of children living with domestic violence and substance misuse should address the specific issue of violence, how it is affected by the use of substances and the impact on parenting capacity. Practitioners should also consider the psychological, emotional and financial impact on the family circumstances of domestic violence and substance misuse when assessing risk to children. The importance of understanding the effects of domestic violence on the behaviour of women is crucial if professionals are to successfully address negative coping strategies (like the misuse of substances) alongside repairing any adverse effects on the relationship with her children. It is by empowering women and making them safe that we best protect children and promote their emotional and physical well being. However we cannot safeguard children without adequately addressing the concerns about women's behaviours as part of any intervention aimed at promoting the safety of women and children.

Definitions of alcohol misuse vary between descriptions of quantity and patterns, to symptoms and effect. Practitioners should ask pertinent questions to ascertain the experience of family members in each particular household. Assumptions should not be made about levels of alcohol required to cause concern. 'Quantity alone is not a sufficient indicator of problem behaviour, people have different reactions to amounts consumed, the way in which the drinking is spread over time is relevant, and sometimes drinking even below the recommended levels has been reported as having an adverse impact on home life' (Tunnard, 2002: 3). McMurran (1999) outlines how the development of violence links with the development of drinking over the lifespan, stating:

> . . . *since generally violent men form one subgroup of perpetrators of domestic violence, this subgroup being more severely violent and characterised by being themselves abused as children, having witnessed parental violence and having high rates of substance use and because witnessing or experiencing violence breeds the next generation of perpetrators of domestic violence it is important to break the cycle by recognising and changing violent individuals as well as preventing further damage to their offspring.*

(p 225)

McMurran concludes that programmes to help parents manage their children effectively, whilst offering support for children to remain committed to school, are important in reducing the effects of alcohol and violence on children's future well being. She advocates that where domestic violence is also concerned, adults should be helped to change their aggressive behaviour whilst children are protected and helped to process their experience. Graham et al. (1998) found that where alcohol was a factor in an incident of domestic violence, it was likely that both parties were intoxicated. Many family circumstances where there are incidents of violence in the home are often more complicated scenarios than that of victim and abuser. Alcohol consumption reduces the ability of adults to resolve difficulties in a reasonable manner. If both adults are drinking heavily the possibility of conflict and violence is heightened. It is important to address the mother's use of alcohol as well as her male partner's use, however for women suffering domestic violence her consumption of alcohol needs to be understood in that context. Indeed, the role of drink for either party should be addressed alongside work on empowering the victim of domestic violence and challenging the distorted mind-set of the abuser (Gordon, 1989).

Practitioners working with families who misuse illegal substances soon become aware of the risk factors posed to family members from the associate drug community. In assessing the potential to change practitioners should be aware that parents may be experiencing abuse, threats and or actual violence from those involved in the procurement of illicit drugs. This may manifest itself in threats of or actual beatings, stabbings, sexual assault and in some cases the use of firearms (Kearney et al., 2005). Violent offences, including murder linked to illicit drug dealing, indicate that the threat of serious harm is very real. For all family members but especially children and young people, experiencing high levels of violence from within and outside the family can lead to the normalisation of this in every day life, especially if the local community reflects similar levels of violence (Kearney et al., 2005). Parents may live in a climate of fear for their safety and the safety of their family. This stress alone and the stress involved in maintaining an expensive drug dependency can lead to reactive violence in the home between parents (Kearney and Taylor 2001). Children of substance users are therefore caught up, by default, in a community of violence where fear influences behaviour and choice.

Practice Scenario 4

Cathy (18 years) had been using heroin and other substances since her early teens. When I met Cathy she was living with her maternal grandparents with her two year daughter. Cathy was closely linked to a wide network of dealers, including her own mother and stepfather. At 16 years old she had started to live with a well known drug 'baron'. During the previous year he had been remanded to prison awaiting trial for large scale drug dealing. Having lived with this man at the time of his arrest and some substances being found in the house they shared, Cathy had been charged with several drug offences. She had been asked to consider giving evidence against her former partner. During the wait for her court date, Cathy became increasingly anxious. She did not want to go to prison herself but felt unable to give evidence against the drug baron for fear of reprisals on her daughter and grandparents. In telling me about the danger she was in she described being held against her will by his associates and threatened that her daughter would be killed if she gave evidence. On another occasion she had been made to watch whilst another youth had been smashed with baseball bats. Although Cathy would spend time talking to me about her safety she was extremely nervous of any suggestions I made to keep her safe. The whole culture of the drug world felt overwhelming to Cathy with little hope of escaping. During this period Cathy's younger sister died of a heroin overdose. Although found alone in a flat, Cathy was convinced she had been deliberately given a potentially toxic strength to kill her. 'I wish you could have done for my sister what you've done for me' Cathy said reflecting on the supportive intervention she had been offered. Over months of work aimed at planning for Cathy's daughter, she decided the best course of action was to refuse to give evidence against her former partner, to take her own punishment and try to break away from the local drug culture on her release. Before going to prison Cathy was able to complete a life story book for her daughter with lots of positive messages about the love she had for her. Maternal grandparents facilitated good contact between Cathy and her daughter during the prison sentence and offered Cathy a home on her release.

At its most extreme children may themselves be threatened or injured as a way of controlling substance misusing parents. Even where this isn't the case, coping with the implied or blatant threats may become part of a way of life for the children of substance users. Some may develop similar bullying strategies in their social relationships, becoming embroiled in community groups were violence is the norm. For others this may extend to the use of intimidation and violence to get their own needs met in close family relationships, especially where those experiences have been reinforced within the context of domestic violence. Whilst the use of many illegal substances will not, in themselves make someone violent, the lifestyle that goes with addiction to illegal substances may well produce tensions in family life that can at times escalate into violence.

The child's experience of domestic violence, alcohol and substance misuse

When assessing the impact on children whose parents are misusing alcohol or substances and are living with domestic violence, no one issue can be assessed without acknowledging the accumulation of disadvantages brought about by adult behaviours. Domestic violence impacts on the parenting capacity of both the abused and the abuser and can lead to dysfunctional coping strategies, parenting style and family norms. It is this relationship between domestic violence, the use of substances as inappropriate coping strategies and the resulting parenting problems that need to be addressed in order to meet the needs of children. A young person's life may well be adversely affected in many areas; their health may be affected by poor housing conditions, inadequate or irregular diet and basic needs consistently left unmet. The young person's attendance at school may be chaotic, resulting in poor achievement, low self-esteem and feeling marginalised. Relationships with their peer group may have been eroded by absence from school or a reduced opportunity to take friends home due to shame or fear that a parent behaves badly. For those families where there are high levels of domestic violence or serious problems brought about by links to a threatening drug community, there may also be the additional difficulties of having to move regularly to escape violent and controlling figures. This may result in broken friendships, disjointed school attendance and isolation. There may be practical difficulties brought about by levels of poverty, poor housing conditions and related health issues, alongside social, emotional and psychological difficulties for both children and adults. In short children and young people living with domestic violence and alcohol or substance misuse may be affected by:

- Insecure home life.
- Attachment difficulties.
- Increased fear of loss and bereavement.
- Psychological difficulties as a result of their experiences.
- Risks of direct abuse to themselves.
- Being included in violence towards family member.
- Feelings of shame and guilt.
- Distorted views on relationships, gender, power and control.
- Distorted views on family life, coping strategies and display of emotions.

Children tell us they are worried about their parents' safety yet feel unable to share their anxiety, because they fear they will make the situation worse. Their concerns can range from real to vicarious dangers. Children often know about levels of drinking, drug use and domestic violence much earlier and in more detail than parents think (Kearney et al., 2005). Callers to help lines report feeling helpless, irritable, nervous, depressed, lonely and anxious. One particular anxiety for young people is that nothing will change and that over time they will behave in the same way as their parents. Without adequate support children may feel despondent and that they have no power to effect change.

Practice Scenario 5

Amy (aged six) was interviewed at school during a Section 47 enquiry relating to her mothers drug dependency and its effects on her parenting. When asked if she had any questions to ask, Amy said 'Why does my mum still take drugs when she knows she shouldn't?' Explaining to Amy in an age appropriate way the difficulties her mother might be experiencing in restricting her use of drugs was important. This helped Amy understand that her mother was not simply being awkward and creating unnecessary problems in the family and helped maintain the positives of their loving relationship.

In relation to alcohol Laybourn et al. (1996) state that children may experience:

- Difficulties in attending school leading to educational failure.
- Feeling marginalised by the education system.
- Arriving late because of parents inability to maintain routine.
- Lack of interest from parents.
- Change of schools due to chaotic lifestyles.
- Poor concentration as a result of anxiety.
- Poor sleep patterns due to chaotic household and listening to violent outbursts.
- Lack of stimulation because parents are under the influence of alcohol or drugs.
- A siphoning off of family resources for alcohol or drugs.

- Promises broken when alcohol becomes priority for cash available and possibly parents using child's belongings or money for alcohol.
- Fear for parents safety because of violence from partner or others.

These are very similar for children living with substance misusing parents and for those living with domestic violence. In the assessment of families where there is domestic violence and substance misuse, professionals should be aware of the significant impact of domestic violence on adult behaviour. Research consistently highlights the adverse effects of living with parental disharmony and the continual threat of violence or family disruption on children's development. Holden (1998) suggests 40 per cent of children from homes where there are levels of domestic violence exhibit clinically significant behavioural problems in comparison to about 10 per cent of children from homes not categorised as violent. Children and young people will exhibit a variety of emotional and behavioural responses depending on their age, level of understanding, resilience, available support networks, extended family strengths and vulnerabilities. Generally children's ability to cope well with adult substance or alcohol misuse is enhanced if there is family harmony and they see parent figures working to meet their child's needs alongside managing their own problem (Cleaver et al., 1999; Velleman and Templeton, Ch. 2). Even when children do not actually witness violent acts they will be affected by overhearing violence, seeing the results of violence and living with highly strained dynamics between parent figures. Children may be aware of high levels of control and intimidation operating between parents which may distort their perceptions regarding the balance of power in relationships and definition of roles and gender in families. The abusive use of power and control may be mirrored in the relationship between parent and child, especially as children grow older and feel able to challenge the authority of their mother. Holden and Ritchie (1991) noted that women who had been physically abused by their partners reported their own inconsistent parenting because of the abuse; difficulties in maintaining standards of care; that child care was regarded as more stressful than other mothers and that some mothers acted in a punitive manner towards their children. It is important that workers help parents to establish a co-operative relationship with their child, reinforcing attachment and helping parent and child experience each other as mutually rewarding. The skills and the comfort of establishing a loving tie with family members should be encouraged with care planning that aims to maintain and promote important relationships for the child. Professionals working with mothers and children (even when those children are placed elsewhere) need to consider ways to enhance the relationship between mother and child, promoting attachment whilst re-enforcing her parental authority. Practitioners need to acknowledge the potential long-term effects of living with domestic violence and misuse alongside other family matters and work to challenge any distorted ideology. This type of work can help reduce the potential of young people moving into adult relationships with dysfunctional notions of family life.

Living with substance misusing parents is likely to have an effect on the child's developing identity and experiencing the domination of women will impact on the developing sense of self. Gender is an important issue for practitioners to address with children of both sexes helping challenge any distorted ideology and helping them understand the balance of power between the sexes. Some children may take on a passive or aggressive role in an attempt to meet the stereotypical demands of their gender role, or to limit the level of violence aimed at them. It is important that workers make attempts to counter balance any negative ideas and challenge any stereotyping of either male or females. Work to promote attachment and to develop the authority and assertiveness of mothers is vital if children are to be cared for by a parent who feels confident. Children need to feel proud of their likeness to either parent as a link to their inheritance and a valuable part of their identity. Boys may feel they will grow up to be like their fathers and this may be reinforced by casual comments from family members. It is important that similarities to an abusive parent relate to the positive aspects of that adult and are given in a manner that boosts the child's developing identity and self-esteem. Children and young people may share similar characteristics or behaviours but they are not their parents. Their life experiences are not the same and they have some choice about present and future behaviour. Children who have experienced parent figures with abusive or addicted behaviours should be encouraged to believe they can make positive choices about their lives, especially how they cope with life's frustrations, express emotion and develop relationships. Experiencing the domination and intimidation of women will affect how boys and girls think about and learn to understand the balance of power between the sexes. Children need positive male influences and the opportunity to see how men and women can live together in relative harmony. Without the experience of positive male figures, often exacerbated whilst living in women-only refuges, it may be very difficult for male children to develop a sense of pride in the positive aspects of being a male member of a family. Refuges, residential care establishments, school and youth services can help promote positive role models by identifying a male mentor to encourage the development of positive male attributes and promote resilience.

Both parent figures can benefit from a better understanding of the impact their behaviour has on their child. Hearing their child's experiences and having an understanding of their child's perception of family life can help motivate parents to change. Episodes of violence recalled by their children can be alarming to adults and especially to parents who have been unaware that their child has known what has been happening. Kelly (1988) and Hester et al. (1995) found many women had decided to leave an abusive partner in response to their child's experience, either because of the child disclosing they were aware of the violence or the direct physical abuse of the child. For those children living with domestic violence the use of alcohol or other substances may well be a trigger, raising anxiety levels in anticipation that violence will later occur. Parents can be helped to understand the triggers for their child by listening to their child's account of life at home. Very often adults will focus on actual incidents of violence or substance misuse not realising the accumulation of anxiety created for the child in what might be every day events. Allowing adult abusers and survivors to hear children's versions of events can be a helpful tool for raising adult's awareness of the reality of domestic violence and substance misuse for children and promote change in either the abusive or abused parent.

Practice Scenario 6

Beth (10 years) had lived with her mother, stepfather and baby sister, but was currently staying with foster carers. She attended group work for children living with domestic violence. During this group work Beth disclosed incidents of heavy alcohol consumption and extreme violence. As part of the agreed intervention I was asked to work directly with Beth alone. In one direct work session Beth talked about seeing her mother stab her stepfather with a kitchen knife. Both adults had been intoxicated at the time. The incident had taken place some three years previously. Her mother had been placed on probation for this attack but had been unaware that Beth had witnessed the incident. On one occasion we talked about the Christmas holidays coming up Beth said, 'I hate Christmas and I don't want to go home for the holidays'. When we explored why, Beth was very clear that in her family Christmas entailed lots of alcohol and this inevitably led to violence. Beth said, 'My mum and dad get drunk and when they get drunk they fight'. The link between socialising, drinking and fear of violence were firmly embedded for Beth: 'he might pull the kitchen cupboards off or my mum might stab him again, I don't want to go'. Her anticipation wasn't focused on the joys of Christmas but being left coping with inappropriate adult behaviours. I was able to feed this information back to those making decisions about her Christmas but more importantly I was able to use this to help her mother understand the impact of past misuse of alcohol and past violence had on Beth. For Beth the fear of violence started long before any actual incident. A change in family behaviour was required in order to reduce the anxiety created by trigger behaviours.

From the child's point of view anxiety often starts at the first sign of parents' drinking or use of a substance that has previously led to violence. The child may become watchful, looking out for behaviours that indicate future problems. The child anticipates that the parent will over-indulge and the excess will lead to violent outbursts. Children living with alcohol misuse will experience anticipatory anxiety even when there is not a violent incident. This sometimes unconscious link is important for alternative carers to understand as even controlled levels of drinking may provoke anxiety in a child who has experienced the adverse effects in the past. For children living with adults who abuse alcohol and become violent the reality is they have little power to affect the deteriorating state of the adult. As the adult continues to drink it is likely that tempers will fray and the tension for the child mounts. Parent figures under the influence of alcohol will be less able to anticipate and meet the needs of children. Children affected by parents' inconsistent behaviour associated with problem drinking (for example chaotic daily routines, poor supervision, ineffectual parenting style, chaotic boundaries and lack of basic household provisions) may take on an adult role with inappropriate control over their parent. The dynamic of the child's attempt to control and subsequent levels of frustration can lead to problems for the parent in managing the child's behaviour. This dysfunctional negative cycle of interaction should be addressed if the parent engages in work to change their substance misuse. As the adult makes progress in changing their behaviours so to must the child adjust to the altering dynamics in the household. As the parent assumes the role of responsive adult with appropriate use of authority, the child is encouraged to feel less responsible for adult issues.

Resilience and protective factors

Children living with substance misuse and domestic violence will have a much greater insight into the fragility of life than other children. The fear for the child of the loss of a parent through hospitalisation, incarceration, separation, divorce, or even death can be constants for children living in high risk families. Children will find it difficult to be comforted by adults who are either emotionally unavailable to them or are violent and intimidating. The child has no safe place and must find internal ways of coping with these powerful feelings. They may well have developed unhealthy coping strategies or developed distorted views on the use of violence or substances as a means of meeting their own needs. Some may resort to self-harm or anti-social behaviour (Laybourn et al., 1996) but not all coping mechanisms are negative. Some studies show more positive interactions between siblings of problem drinkers compared with children in the control groups (Velleman and Orford, 1999). Research in families where there are significant alcohol problems advises identifying and promoting the following protective factors for children:

- A stable relationship with a non-drinking parent or other adult.
- Nurturing from others within the family.
- Active use of an informal network outside the family for advice and assistance.
- Parents providing structure and control including a united and caring front, family activities and time and attention.
- Positive influences at school.
- The maintenance of self-esteem and coping skills in the child, including an acquired sense of the meaning and faith about life.

The importance of assessing the child's resilience, safety factors in the family network and effectiveness of service provision are as important as assessing levels of danger to the child. Children's services aimed at promoting independence, assertiveness and resilience have much to offer children living with adult based difficulties. Building children's ability to cope with adversity is vital if we are to leave children in families where adults are dependent on substance and are violent. Rutter (1985) outlined the key components of resilience as:

- A sense of self-esteem and self-confidence.
- A belief in one's self-efficacy and ability to deal with change and adaptation.
- A repertoire of social problem solving approaches.

Disinhibiting aspects of substances

Children living with violent and intimidating adults quickly learn that in order to remain safe, one person's needs take priority over your own. Even children who have their basic needs met may have learned powerful lessons about hierarchy and power in the family system. By consistently witnessing the abuse of one parent, children are also warned of the consequences of speaking out against the perpetrator and the harsh consequences of their misuse of power. In such circumstances the child who is then directly abused is unlikely to feel able to alert the safe parent for fear of reprisals. Adults who are unable to place their children's safety as a priority, either because of their own substance use or intimidation, leave their children vulnerable to various types of abuse. The use of drugs and alcohol can seriously affect parenting style and ability to meet the needs of children. The disinhibiting aspects of substances can lower tolerance levels, heighten frustrations and for some exacerbate any tendencies towards violence. Boundaries for behaviour can be more easily breached whilst under the influence of substances. These may include becoming violent to a partner or child and other direct abuses of children such as sexual abuse. Araji and Finkelhor (1986) and McMurran (1999) found that alcohol and other drugs lowered the inhibitions that keep people from acting upon physically or sexually violent impulses. Hayes and Emshoff (1993) found that additional difficulties experienced by substance misusers (such as sexual problems caused by the physical effects of substances) or the rejection of an addict's advances by adults, may result in stress that manifests itself in physical or sexual violence towards a spouse or child. Feelings of guilt and shame may be diminished whilst under the influence of substances, minimising negative consequences of abusive behaviour. Misusing substances can tip the balance between adequate and abusive parenting. Practitioners should be clear how different substances are affecting the thought processes of adults and may require help from substance misuse services working with the adult to identify areas of concern. In a study of 295 suspected child maltreatment cases Tominson (1994) found an alcohol problem was identified for at least one adult in the family in 16.9 per cent of the sexual abuse cases; 40 per cent of the physical abuse cases; 31.3 per cent of emotional abuse cases and 28 per cent of the neglect cases. A drug problem was identified in 6.45 per cent of sexual abuse cases; 16.7 per cent of physical abuse cases and 41.3 per cent of neglect cases. Cleaver et al. (1999) discovered that when a visit was made as a result of child protection referral the rate of familial domestic violence stood at 40 per cent.

Being brought up by aggressive or intoxicated adults may result in the child experiencing an inconsistent parenting style with periods of poor supervision and unmet needs. This may run in conjunction with a harsh style of discipline and punishment. Children used to seeing their parent beaten or intimidated quickly learn the power of using fear or physical force to get your needs met. McMurran (1999: 221) states 'under such circumstances the child is unlikely to learn to control their own behaviour and experiences harshness as a means of behavioral control . . . the children begin to see the world as antagonistic towards them'. Family violence and substance misuse often restrict relationships and social activities outside the home, with children left to socialise with other substance misusing families. This will reinforce the normality of the lifestyle providing unhelpful models of adult behaviour to be emulated by children and young people. Substances may lower the threshold for aggression and violence and will act as a disinhibitor for a variety of behaviours not conducive with adequate parenting, i.e. embarrassing displays of bravado, sexually explicit behaviour, arguing and threats of violence. Living with high levels of violence and intimidation from within the family and the community may result in distorted notions of appropriate behaviour. Both adults and children require their individual needs to be met simultaneously in order to co-ordinate the resolution of difficulties at a personal level, whilst providing additional support aimed at maintaining positive changes throughout the family system. However most services aim at one particular problem with an emphasis on adult or child services only. In reality children are often left managing the care of parents or acting as substitute carer for siblings whilst the adults problem behaviour remains entrenched. For many children even when living with the complexity of domestic violence and substance misuse they will not provoke a full child protection intervention. Effective family support needs to confidently highlight areas of work required for family safety and focus intervention on specific areas including adult service based interventions. Some children's services may feel they lack the authority of child protection agencies to gain co-operation from adult services in a co-ordinated family support package:

> if all we possess in our threshold 'toolkit' is the 'hammer' of child protection, then we tend to respond to every demand as though it is a nail, when often it may be a screw, a tack or even a drawing pin!

(Calder and Hackett, 2003: 359)

Early intervention may well prevent crises points or the escalation of unmet need to a point of serious child protection concern. Workers from all agencies charged with the task of safeguarding children should assess all aspects of family life and their impact on the child, targeting appropriate services to specific areas of vulnerability. However it may become necessary to place children away from the family home. For children subject to care proceedings domestic violence was a factor in 51 per cent of cases coming to court (Hunt et al., 2000). The safety of the child is often achieved with some cost in severing ties with familiar people and places. This in itself brings for the child a period of traumatic adjustment and anxiety, which may end with permanent removal from both parents.

Practice Scenario 7

After weeks of individual work Ebony (nine years) asked to see her mother to tell her some of her thoughts about being in foster care. Her mother had frequently told Ebony that she loved her and wanted her home as soon as possible. Ebony knew her mother was also working with me to address issues of domestic violence and alcohol misuse. Ebony said to her mother 'Let's face it mum you've chose him over me, if you really wanted me back home you would ask him to leave and stop drinking so much'. This was a turning point for Ebony and her mother in that it highlighted how Ebony had interpreted her mother's decision making and her struggle to end an abusive relationship and its affect on their continued relationship. Understanding that Ebony felt her mother was rejecting her, despite continued verbal confirmation of her love, motivated this mother to make significant changes to her life.

Support services

Providing support to families in this situation requires an holistic package of support linking adults with specialist services aimed at reducing their behaviour, whilst offering services to the child or young person aimed at building resilience and safety. Bancroft et al. (2004) found that many young people in their study said they had had no support from services. However for those who had received support, a strong relationship with a service worker seemed to contribute to resilience. The young people identified being flexible, having an informal manner, having a forward looking approach and an understanding, non-critical attitude towards their parents as important qualities in supporters. Many support service staff already provide high levels of these person centred skills when working with children and young people in need. A more co-ordinated holistic intervention focussing on both child and adults' needs would enhance this intervention. Significantly young people did not always want to talk about feelings or experiences, being allowed some space from their experiences in the home. This ought to reduce workers' anxieties regarding what might be seen as 'specialist intervention', indeed it is the consistent, positive regard for individuals provided in the context of age appropriate activities from which children and young people benefit.

Kearney et al. (2003) found that the focus on 'child protection training' across services does little to promote the idea of family support at an early stage by a co-ordinated response from adult and children's services. They state this emphasis:

. . . can mean adult services see their involvement with families as only coming into play where there are child protection concerns, and often only when these are understood as serious requiring formal action under legislation and procedures. Working with the whole family may become synonymous with high professional anxiety and statutory action.

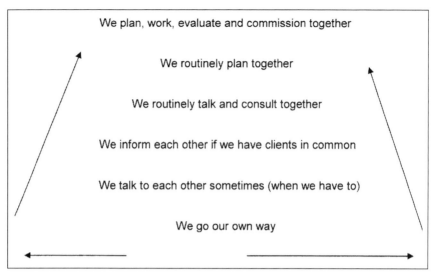

We plan, work, evaluate and commission together

We routinely plan together

We routinely talk and consult together

We inform each other if we have clients in common

We talk to each other sometimes (when we have to)

We go our own way

Figure 1　Pyramid of co-operation (Murphy and Oulds, 2000: 115)

Relationships need to be developed across services to reduce this level of anxiety, increase the level of confidence and knowledge in each services' expertise and eventually promote joint planning, commissioning and evaluating of services. Murphy and Oulds (2000) pyramid of co-operation helps us identify where our local services may be and provides useful targets for service development.

Conclusion

This chapter has considered the complexity of dual and triple concern in families and the impact on children and young people. It has considered some of the research on each of the specific areas of substance misuse, alcohol addiction and the overlap with domestic violence. Those who work with families know that we may encounter violence, substance misuse and or excessive use of alcohol in the same family. It is this cross-over of adult behaviour and its impact on the lives of children that poses complex and challenging dilemmas to children and practitioners. Children and young people, who live with high levels of violence and fear, are inevitably adversely affected by their experiences. Research suggests that both parental domestic violence and substance misuse individually increase the level of risk posed to children not only of immediate significant harm, but of longer-term negative consequences. If the two factors are experienced together the danger is compounded and consequently the risk of harm is significantly increased. Parents experiencing difficulties in meeting the needs of their children due to their own behaviour, will find it difficult to acknowledge the problem and ask for help. Shame and embarrassment (alongside genuine fear that their children will be removed from their care), block access to services, leaving both adult and child isolated from effective support. This chapter has emphasised that adult services need to work more closely with children's services, acknowledging the overlap between parents' individual need and those of their children. It is likely that even when parents seek help for their own problem behaviour, intervention will focus on the presenting problem and not the underlying factors nor the impact on other family members. Whilst, in the best adult provision, some type of holistic risk assessment may take place, most adult drug and alcohol services are not resourced to offer work aimed at the promotion of positive parenting and the attachment between adult and child. Without sufficient links with children's services this leaves many children without the intervention required to affect change in their family circumstances.

The cross-over of responsibility lies with both adult and child focussed services. For their part practitioners in children's services need to be able to identify what resources are available to best meet the needs of adults, and how to monitor the effect of such services on parenting capacity. Adult services need to be informed about what can be provided for the children of their clients and how best to link with family support and safeguarding services to ensure children are not left vulnerable. At this time of radical change in children's services it is timely to consider how the needs of young people living in violent homes where there are also significant alcohol or drug problems can be addressed. Whilst much has been done to improve joint working with Community Drug Teams there is still some way to go to develop joint working protocols with alcohol services. A closer link would allow for a similar level of co-operative working. However it is not enough to advocate improved working together at the point of child protection crises, indeed much can be done to prevent significant harm at an earlier stage. Adult drug and alcohol services have much to offer children service workers sharing their knowledge and expertise regarding effective interventions. Children's service staff can help adult teams to identify risk factors for children and young people living with users and to provide support, including individual work where required. Closer working between alcohol and drug teams with children's services can help establish a network of supportive resources offered routinely to family members when an adult seeks help. When Community Drug Teams developed close working relationships with child protection services, both have benefited from the other's knowledge and skills. When it works well, holistic supportive interventions linking adult's needs with those of their children are the norm. Some Community Drug Teams will have social workers based on site offering assessment and support to service user's families. A similar approach in alcohol services would be most effective.

The separation of adult and children's services which may be exaggerated by the move to mental health trusts and children's trusts may make such developments more difficult. Unless local authorities identify gaps in service provision and seek to address these, they may well be lost in the flurry to achieve current government set targets for national change within a tight time frame. This chapter has advocated that as part of the development of multi-disciplinary teams, Safeguarding Boards should consider employing alcohol and substance misuse staff in children's services working alongside social workers and health visitors. Such a multi-disciplinary team could offer advice, support and ensure appropriate resources were delivered when required. Similarly children family support workers could work within adult alcohol and drug services, highlighting the needs of children, assessing levels of risk and advocating on behalf of vulnerable children to ensure appropriate intervention. Whilst advocating cross service provision I acknowledge the enormity of the task, realising it will take time to embed such a cultural and strategic change across very different service provision. True collaboration requires clear protocols, joint strategic planning and incremental development of relationships and understanding of each other's role across agencies. This chapter recognises that front line workers are already trying to work across such barriers in an attempt to promote the care of children by their parents.

References

Abrahams, C. (1994) *The Hidden Victims: Children and Domestic Violence*. London: NCH.

ACMD (2003) *Hidden Harm: Responding to the Needs of Children of Problem Drug Users*. London: HMSO.

Alcohol Concern (2001) *Alcohol and the Family*. Information Bulletin 3rd May.

Araji, G. and Finkelhor, D. (1986) Abusers: A Review of the Research. In Finkelhor, D. *A Sourcebook on Child Sexual Abuse*. Beverly Hills: Sage.

Bancroft, A. et al. (2004) *Parental Drug and Alcohol Misuse: Resilience and Transition Among Young People*. Joseph Rowntree Foundation.

Brandon, M. and Lewis, A. (1996) Significant Harm and Children's Experiences of Domestic Violence. *Child and family Social Work*. 1: 1, 33–42.

Bridge Child Care Consultancy (1991) *Sukina: An Evaluation Report of the Circumstances Leading to her Death*. London: Bridge Child Care Consultancy Service.

Brisbay, T., Baker, S. and Hedderwick, T. (1997) *Under the Influence: Coping With Parents Who Drink Too Much*. London: Alcohol Concern.

Calder, M.C. (Ed.) (2005) *Children and Young People Who Sexually Abuse: New Theory, Research and Practice Developments*. Lyme Regis: Russell House Publishing.

Calder, M. with Harold, G. and Howarth, E. (2004) *Children Living With Domestic Violence*. Lyme Regis: Russell House Publishing.

Calder, M.C. and Hackett, S. (2003) *Assessment in Child Care: Using and Developing Frameworks for Practice*. Lyme Regis: Russell House Publishing.

Cleaver, H. and Freeman, P. (1995) *Parental Perspectives in Cases of Suspected Child Abuse*. London: HMSO.

Cleaver, H., Unell, I. and Aldgate, J. (1999) *Children's Needs: Parenting Capacity*. London: HMSO.

Crawford, M. and Garner, R. (1991) *Women Killing: Intimate Femicide in Ontario 1974–1990*. Toronto, ON: Women We Honour Action Committee.

DfES (2005) *Government Response to Hidden Harm.* London: HMSO.

DHSS (1994) *Report of the Committee of Inquiry Into the Care and Supervision Provided in Relation to Maria Colwell.* London: HMSO.

Dobash, R.E. and Dobash, R.P. (1992) *Women, Violence and Social Change.* London: Routledge.

DoH (1995a) *Child Protection: Messages From Research.* London: HMSO.

Farmer, E. and Owen, M. (1995) *Child Protection Practice: Private Risks and Public Remedies.* London: HMSO.

Forrester, D. (2000) Parental Substance Abuse and Child Protection in a British sample. *Child Abuse Review.* 9, 235–46.

Gordon, L. (1989) *Heroes of Their Own Lives.* London: Virago.

Graham, K. et al. (1998) Current Directions in Research on Understanding and Preventing Intoxicated Aggression. *Addiction.* 93: 659–76.

Hamer, M. (2005) *Preventing Breakdown.* Lyme Regis: Russell House Publishing.

Harbin, F. (2001) *The Connaught Square Safer Families Project.* Conference Paper 7.12.

Harbin, F. and Murphy, M. (2000) *Substance Misuse and Child Care. How to Understand, Assist and Intervene When Drugs Affect Parenting.* Lyme Regis: Russell House Publishing.

Harwin, J. and Forrester, D. (2005) *Parental Substance Misuse and Child Welfare.* London: Nuffield.

Hayes, H.R. and Emshoff, J.G. (1993) Dynamics of Alcoholic Families. In Estes, N.J. and Heinemann, M.N. (Eds.) *Alcoholism: Developmental, Consequencies and Interventions.* CV Mosby.

Hester, M. et al. (1995) *Women, Violence and Male Power.* Milton Keynes: Open University Press.

Hester, M., Pearson, C. and Harwin, N. (2000) *Making an Impact: Children and Domestic Violence. A Reader.* London: Jessica Kingsley.

Holden, G.W. (1998) Introduction: The Development of Research Into Another Consequence of Family Violence. In Holden, G.W., Geffner, R. and Jouriles, E.N. (Eds.) *Children Exposed to Marital Violence: Theory, Research and Applied Issues.*

Holden, G.W. and Ritchie, K.L. (1991) Linking Extreme Marital Discord, Child Rearing and Child Behaviour Problems: Evidence From Battered Women. *Child Development.* 62: 311–27.

Home Office (2000) *British Crime Survey England and Wales.* London: Home Office.

Home Office (2001) *British Crime Survey England and Wales.* London: Home Office.

Houston, A., Kork, S. and MacLeod, M. (1997) *Beyond the Limit: Children Who live With Parental Alcohol Misuse.* London: Childline.

Hunt, J. et al. (2000) *The Last Resort: Child Protection, the Courts and the 1989 Children Act.* London: HMSO.

Islington Area Child Protection Committee (1989) *Review of the Circumstances of the Death of Liam Johnson.* Islington: Islington ACPC.

Kearney, J. and Taylor, N. (2001) *The Highs and Lows of Family Life*. University of Salford.

Kearney, J., Harbin, F., Murphy, M., Wheeler, E and Whittle, J. (2005) *The Highs and Lows of Family Life: Familial Substance Misuse From a Child's Perspective*. Bolton Substance Misuse Research Group.

Kearney, P., Levin, E. and Rosen, G. (2000) *Working With Families With Alcohol, Drug and Mental Health Problems*. London: NISW.

Kearney, P., Levin, E. and Rosen, G. (2003) *Alcohol, Drug and Mental Health Problems: Working With Families*. SCIE.

Kelley, L. (1988) *Surviving Sexual Violence*. Cambridge: Policy Press.

Laybourn, A., Brown, J. and Hill, M. (1996) *Hurting on the Inside: Children's Experiences of Parental Alcohol Misuse*. Aldershot: Avebury.

London Borough of Greenwich (1987) *A Child in Mind: Protection of Children in Responsible Society. Report of the Commission of Inquiry into the Circumstances Surrounding the Death of Kimberley Carlile*. London Borough of Greenwich.

McMurran, M. (1999) Alcohol and Violence. *Child Abuse Review*. 8: 219–30.

McNeil, M. (1987) Domestic Violence: The Skeleton in Toprasoff's Closet. In Sonkin, D.J. (Ed.) *Domestic Violence Trial: Psychological and Legal Dimensions of Family Violence*. New York: Springer.

Mirrlees-Black, C. (1999) *British Crime Survey*. Research Study No132. London: HMSO.

Mullender, A. and Humphries, C. (1998) *Domestic Violence and Child Abuse: Policy and Practice Issues for Local Authorities and Other Agencies*. London: Local Government Association.

Murphy, M. and Oulds, G. (2000) Establishing and Developing Co-operative Links between Substance Misuse and Child Protection Systems. In Harbin, F. and Murphy, M. (Eds) *Substance Misuse and Childcare*. Lyme Regis: Russell House Publishing.

NCB (1993) *Investigation into Inter-agency Practice Concerning the Death of Toni Dales*. London: NCB.

NCH (1994) *The Hidden Victims: Children and Domestic Violence*. London: NCH.

O'Hara, M. (1994) *Child Deaths in the Context of Domestic Violence: Implications for Professional Practice*. In Mullender, A. and Morley, R. (Eds.) *Children Living With Domestic Violence: Putting Men's Abuse of Women on the Child Care Agenda*. London: Whiting and Birch.

Reder, P. and Duncan, S. (1999) *Lost Innocents: A Follow up Study of Fatal Child Abuse*. London: Routledge.

Rowsell, C. (2001) Presentation to Relate National Conference 3rd April as cited in Calder, M.C. (2005) *Children Living with Domestic Violence*. Lyme Regis: Russell House Publishing.

Rutter, M. (1985) Resilience in the Face of Adversity. Protective Factors and Resistance to Psychiatric Disorder. *British Journal of Psychiatry*. 147: 598–611.

Stark, E. and Flitcraft, A. (1988) Women and Children at Risk: A Feminist Perspective on Child Abuse. *International Journal of Health Studies*. 18.

Thompson, A.E. and Blennerhassett, R. (1996) Mental Health Needs for Children of Parents Seeking Help for Substance Abuse. *Psychiatric Bulletin.* 20, 137–9.

Tominson, A.M. (1994) *An Evaluation of Decision Making in Child Abuse Services in the Barwon Region: A Report for the Victorian Health Promotion Foundation.* Melbourne: Monash University.

Tunnard, J. (2002) Parental Problem Drinking and Its Impact on Children. *Research in Practice: Research Reviews.* January.

Velleman, R. (1993) *Alcohol and the Family.* Institute of Alcohol Studies.

Velleman, R. and Orford, J. (1993) The Importance of Family Discord in Explaining Childhood Problems *Addiction Research.* 1: 1, 39–57.

Velleman, R. and Orford, J. (1999) *Risk and Resilience: Adults Who Were the Children of Problem Drinkers.* Harwood Academic Publishers.

West, M. and Prinz, R. (1987) Parental Alcoholism and Childhood Psychopathy. *Psychological Bulletin,* 102, 204–18.

Yearnshire, S. (1997) Analysis of Cohort. In Bewley, S., Friend, J. and Mezey, G. (Eds.) *Violence Against Women.* London: RCOG.

Chapter 6

The Roller Coaster of Change: The Process of Parental Change from a Child's Perspective

Fiona Harbin

Introduction

What we as adults may accept as the process of change (Prochaska and DiClemente, 1992) the young people sometimes found more emotionally traumatic than the problem itself.

(*The Highs and Lows of Family Life*, Kearney et al. (2005))

This claim followed a series of research interviews with young people on their perceptions of living with drug use. It came as a surprise that what we as adults see as a positive process of change, could be perceived by the children as so traumatic. During the research this concept was called the 'roller coaster of change', a title that summed up the ups and downs of the experience for the young people, which seemed to be in stark contrast to the ideal of the flowing cycle of change that their parents may have been experiencing. When working with families affected by substances, knowing how children might experience change will inevitably have a fundamental impact on how we approach parental change more sensitively, and how we help children make sense of it.

This chapter will look at the accepted stages of adult behavioural change, specifically relating to parental substance misuse and then deconstruct these stages to consider how a child or young person may experience this. It will examine helpful models of change and consider how practitioners can utilise these and ease the process of parental change for children and young people.

The need for change

None of us will avoid change in our lives. It is an ongoing process that enables us to develop as individuals and moves us from one stage of our lives to the next. Change may be as simple as choosing a new brand of toothpaste or as difficult as deciding to end a long-term relationship. The degree of ease or difficulty of these changes or transitions will depend on the internal factors and external factors of the individual and their environment.

The idea of change and the individual's ability to change underpins our work with children in need. Without the strong belief that change is possible, much work in this field would be seen as futile or even unethical. Our assessments often lead to interventions based on facilitating and measuring change, to ensure the safety and well being of children in their families. This is particularly apparent when working with parental substance misuse.

As discussed in Chapter 1, not all parents who misuse substances are unable to provide adequate care for their children but many may, on occasion, need extra support. We know that, because of parental substance misuse and its potential negative impact in some families, children may not be cared for adequately, consistently or safely.

Good practice dictates that each family should be assessed separately and assumptions should not be made just because parents are misusing substances (SCODA, 1997; Cleaver et al., 1999). However, research indicates some common themes when looking at the impact of parental substance misuse on the child (Alison, 2000; Kearney, 2005). This lengthy list includes lack of provision of basic needs; regular accidental injuries; age inappropriate levels of responsibility for self, siblings and parents; emotional unavailability of a parent; attachment problems; behavioural problems and conduct disorder; substance misuse; exposure to drug use and violence; stigma; separation and loss and an unpredictable lifestyle. This list is by no means exhaustive and many children will be experiencing one or more of these effects.

When considering these potential effects we will want to help the child and the family in order to improve their situation. To do this, adult behavioural change is essential (Murphy et al., 1991) and in this case the parent must start to address and change their substance misuse. McKeganey et al. (2002) found in their sample of currently drug-free parents, that their drug use had affected all aspects of their children's lives, but when substance misuse was addressed, this led to family circumstances improving dramatically. Research (Murphy et al., 1991) indicates than none of the concerns about parenting improve if there is no significant change in the parent's use of substances.

For many parents substance misuse may only be one of many problems or may be a means of them dealing with these other problems. However, from a child's perspective, parents need to change their substance misuse as soon as possible or an inadequate situation may not only continue but may also deteriorate.

Many practitioners will have asked parents to consider change around their substance use and will have advised an appointment at the local substance service. Because of the necessary emphasis on parental change, engagement at the substance misuse service is seen as a positive step for all the family. For the children it signifies a hope that there will be an improvement in the near future and for the parent it is the start of a long therapeutic journey. This journey may not only address issues of substance misuse but often personal issues which have been blocked out by regular substance misuse.

In situations where there are serious concerns regarding a child's well being, the decision making process often hinges on the parents' engagement with treatment services. It is at this stage that children and young people have said their circumstances become more difficult.

Those children interviewed indicated that there was an acceptance of and familiarity with their parent's pre-change state that, however risky it appeared to the outsider, was the norm to those living in the household. This familiar way of life was shattered when the change process began. Once change had begun, parents would experience a wide range of emotions from hope to despair as they travelled through the stages of the cycle, with periods of stability regularly followed by relapse. For the adults, this was acceptable progress on the road to change, for the children this was an emotional roller coaster of unpredictability, underpinned with self-blame, broken promises and uncertainty.

Change cycles

There is much literature on the nature of change and the facilitation of change (Prochaska and DiClemente, 1982; Miller and Rollnick, 1991; Hamer, 2005). In this well researched field, much consideration is given to the difficulty of changing behaviour, in particular overcoming a dependency on a substance. As a therapeutic aid for the worker and the client Prochaska and DiClemente developed a wheel of change. The diagram below shows a wheel of change based on the one developed by Prochaska and DiClemente (1982)

Appropriate adult interventions are detailed in the many adult treatment guides, and therefore this chapter will briefly cover this aspect of adult intervention. But we will discuss in much more detail the interventions we can offer the children of those adults. At each stage we will consider the adult change process in order to reveal the impact of this on a child.

Pre-contemplation

This adapted wheel of change begins at the pre-contemplative stage. At this stage the parent sees no need to change and has not recognised that they have a problem. This may be the parent who denies to the worker that they are using amphetamine, for example. The worker may see the signs of dependence and others may have told you that this parent uses stimulants. You have asked appropriately about the use of substances but are faced with denial. This parent may, for many reasons, not wish to disclose their use. These may include the fear of children being placed on the child

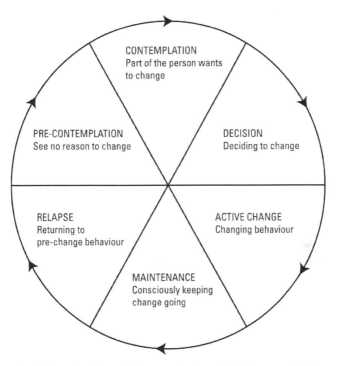

Figure 2   The adult cycle: adapted from Prochaska and DiClemente, 1982

protection register, or taken into care (Elliot and Watson, 1998), being judged a bad parent and having to address difficult issues which have been masked by substance misuse (Kearney, 2001). These are significant barriers, especially to mothers, to disclosing their substance misuse. However, some will genuinely believe that they are in control of their substance misuse, and that it is not having a substantial impact on their life, therefore there is no need to change.

Confrontation at this stage for many parents may lead to defensiveness and aggression (Miller and Rollnick, 1991; Hamer, 2005). Therefore any intervention must be sensitive to this whilst ensuring an open dialogue about your concerns as a worker.

Contemplation

The next stage on this cycle is the contemplation stage, whereby the parent begins to recognise and regret the impact their dependence is having on themselves, their lifestyle or their family. However, this can be an ambivalent state and the parent has not yet decided to change. This may be the parent who is struggling financially to maintain a heroin dependency and who can see that their ability to provide for their child's basic needs has been suffering. At the same time this parent may justify their behaviour by comparing it favourably to many of their friends and thinking of the times when they have provided well for their children.

During this period a parent may be more susceptible to advice, guidance and information and may benefit from many of the therapeutic change interventions, most notably motivational interviewing and solution focused work.

Decision

There may be one or more events or incidents that lead to a parent making a decision to change. For some women pregnancy may be the catalyst for changing their drug using behaviour (Macrory and Harbin, 2000). Many of us have changed our behaviour, specifically relating to drinking alcohol and smoking cigarettes, at the news of pregnancy. For others the drug related death of someone close, imprisonment, health worries, the fear of involvement with child care agencies, or a specific incident where their child has suffered can be enough to tip the balance in favour of change. Then there will be others who chose change as the next stage in their lives for no immediate apparent reason apart from the cumulative effects of years of misuse:

> *I just had to stop (using drugs) 'cos I didn't want my daughter to go without and have a dad who was a junkie and a thief. I had to do it for my wife and my parents as well 'cos they deserved more than all that shit.*

> (George (Elliot and Watson, 1998))

Whatever the reason, this is a significant step in the process of changing the substance misusing behaviour. As with any stage of the cycle the parent may slip back to the previous stage, making it vital that those involved with the parents offer as much support and advice as possible on the most appropriate way forward.

Active change

Depending on the services available in the locality, this will usually mean parents attending the local statutory drug or alcohol team, substance misuse service, or a specific voluntary project. Many parents will make this appointment themselves, and others with some encouragement. But for some parents the appointment will have been made for them and they will have been expected to attend, having been told that failure to do so will be criticised in the assessment of their parenting capacity and their commitment to change. To attend an appointment in itself, for whatever reason, can be seen as a positive step towards change. Brief therapy recognises the importance of pre-session change and suggests that even coerced clients can benefit from the therapeutic input, and their behaviour may change as a result.

Whatever brings the parent to their first appointment, it is likely that a complete detoxification programme or a programme of alternate prescribing will be advised. For the parent this may mean a period away from home, some severe physical withdrawal symptoms, psychological disturbance, and the stress associated with major change.

Maintenance

The maintenance stage is where the changes made in the initial stages are maintained. Often a parent will already be drug free or will be on a maintenance prescription monitored by the treatment service. The initial detoxification is by no means the hardest part of the change process. It is during the maintenance stage that many parents will have to work hard at putting the pieces back in to their lives that were lost when they were dependent. This often means learning to parent, and re-building a damaged relationship with a child and other family members. A parent may also be dealing with past physical or psychological trauma which has been masked by the use of substances, often since childhood.

To maintain abstinence or life on a prescribed alternative, ongoing support is vital, and many may feel that they never exit the cycle but remain permanently in the maintenance stage, working hard not to return to their previous lifestyle.

Relapse

There are many triggers which may cause a minor lapse or a major relapse:

It just wasn't as easy as I thought it would be. If I could have got away from here and done it, I probably would have been all right, but it is just too easy to walk over the bridge or get somebody to meet you and score.

(Anon (Elliot and Watson, 1998))

When your life has been dominated by substances it is obvious why Prochaska and DiClemente identified that relapse was an expected stage. They indicated that of those attempting to change, most went round the wheel three to seven times with an average of four cycles.

There are many relapse prevention techniques and interventions used by the drug and alcohol services, but it is important that adults entering into the cycle understand that relapse is inevitable and should not be seen as failure. Without this information parental behaviour following a relapse may be more detrimental to the family than the relapse itself.

Practice Scenario 1

Monica, stabilised on a methadone prescription, had one daughter in care. She was working towards her returning home. After relapsing (using heroin with her ex-partner) she did not attend any appointments for two months. She said later that she had let everybody down and believed that she had ruined any chance of her daughter returning so she had decided not to contact those involved. Her absence from appointments, and the deterioration in her circumstances that ensued, had a more detrimental impact on her case in the family court, than would the one relapse she experienced.

Following a relapse at any stage of the cycle the individual can re-enter the cycle. It is unlikely that the client would re-enter the pre-contemplative sector, returning instead to contemplation. Some may re-enter immediately to a stage further round the cycle. Each time the cycle is entered it becomes slightly less difficult, the client benefits from their previous experiences. This can be likened to a spiral of ever decreasing circles, cumulating in the point of change, see Figure 2.

Timescales

There is no fixed timescale for this cycle and clients involved with adult treatment services will not be expected to change by a certain date but instead at their own pace. However, children do have developmental and risk timescales which as practitioners we cannot ignore. Our planning and work with families has to be based on the children's needs and their own timetables and it is at this point that the divergence of the adult and child's needs become more and more apparent.

The child's cycle

The change cycle is an excellent method of encapsulating the process of change. It is a helpful tool of explanation and can aid the identification of appropriate resources dependent on the stage in the cycle (Hamer, 2005). This permissive cycle, with a pace dictated by the individual, may serve as a guide for individual self-motivated change. However, for parents who misuse substances it is usually interpreted in an adult focused way with a disregard for those who are waiting and experiencing the process of change from a very different, child's perspective (Hogan and Higgins, 2001).

During the assessment process, we need to be mindful of the conflict of different timescales involved between parental change processes and a child's need for safety and stability. The age of the child, the existing attachment, the potential for maintaining change and the child's placement whilst parental change takes place, all need to be taken into account. There will be a point where change has happened to everyone's satisfaction or where a child's need for immediate stability and/or safety outweighs the benefits of living with a regularly relapsing parent. From a practitioner's perspective, this is a difficult area of work where decision making is rarely clear cut and thresholds are often blurred (Walker and Beckett, 2003).

Whilst practitioners struggle to make the best plans for children in these circumstances, the young people interviewed in recent research (Kearney et al., 2005) indicated that there are, for them, many other difficulties implicit in their parent's attempts at change. These difficulties are not always recognised by the adults involved. Based on what the young people indicated we can begin to build up an outer ring to the accepted process of change which explores the stages in the cycle from the child's point of view.

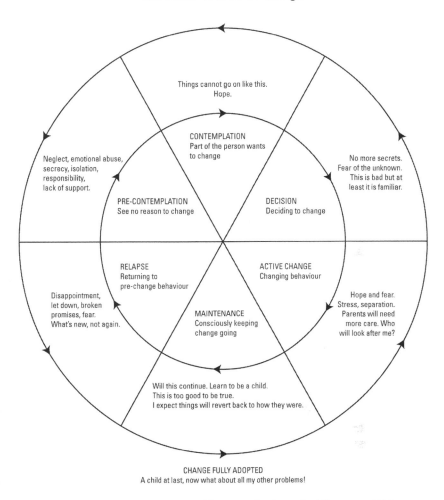

Figure 3 Child's change cycle: adapted from Prochaska and DiClemente, 1982

Pre-contemplation

The parent at this stage is denying their problem and sees no need to change their substance misusing lifestyle. However, for the child this can be a time of secrecy and fear. The parental substance misuse may have been successfully hidden for years and the child may fear the circumstances of this being disclosed. From the child's point of view the potential repercussions may be separation from their parents due to imprisonment or being taken away to live in 'care'.

The child or young person may also be experiencing some of the potential neglect issues commonly associated with parental substance misuse (see Chapter 1). In this case the child may be caring for themselves, their siblings and possibly their parent. The child's experience of being parented is likely to be unpredictable, their basic needs may not be being regularly met, emotional warmth may be reduced, they may be exposed to threatening and violent behaviour, they may witness or have access to drug taking and drug paraphernalia, they may already be living with extended family or have been separated from their parents through imprisonment or hospitalisation and they may be isolated from their peers and stigmatised at school or in the local community (Kearney et al., 2005).

Despite the potential signs of danger in this situation apparent to a concerned adult, for some children this pre-change state, in retrospect, will look more favourable than some of the circumstances they experience at latter stages in the cycle.

In many ways the children and young people became accustomed to this lifestyle and there was a sense that the unpredictable became the familiar.

(Kearney et al., 2005: 21)

Contemplation

As the parent moves to the contemplation stage and begins thinking about change, it is not difficult to imagine how the child feels. An anticipation of change for the better, a hope that their current situation can now improve, or a tinge of fear of the unknown, may be growing in the child's imagination.

It is at this stage that we begin to see how the cycle differs for the child. The parent may revisit this stage several times whilst striving to make changes. With each visit, the process becomes a little easier as some contemplative thought processes have already taken place. However, from a child's perspective a return to this stage will not signify a move forward but a return to how things were. They will no longer feel the same optimism and the same hope, and the fear of the unknown may increase as the child realises the difficulties implicit in parental change.

Decision

This is an important step for the parent and signifies a determination to make changes in their behaviour. Likewise for the child, this signifies a time of hope, anticipation, and fear of what changes are going to take place. It is at this stage that children may begin to feel responsible for their parent's success on their road to change. Because of the impact of parental substance misuse on all aspects of family life (Mahoney and MacKechnie, 2001) children and young people recognise their involvement as a factor in the decision making process.

A second and third visit to this stage by the parent could lead to their children over-internalising their own behaviour and the impact this had on their parents need to revisit this stage (Kearney et al., 2005).

Active change

This can be a very exciting time for a child. Again they may experience anticipation of a positive outcome and be hopeful for their future. However, many young people will be taking on caring responsibilities for their parents, both practically and emotionally. For a child who already worries about their parent's well being a potential period of physical withdrawal symptoms and physical or psychological ill health may be extremely stressful. For this child the caring role may increase as their parent takes the difficult steps towards change. Alternatively, some young people may experience short term separation from their families at this stage, as some parents are admitted to hospitals or detox units, or undergo home detox which may require the child to stay with friends or relatives.

During this stage hopes are high as the parent reduces or ceases use of a substance, which may have been identified as the cause of problems within the family for many years. This is a fragile time and moving on to the next stage of the cycle is not always inevitable.

Practice Scenario 2

Shaun, a heroin user, was admitted to a residential detox unit over 200 miles from home. His son, David aged 18 months, remained with his mother, Debbie, who was just beginning methadone treatment. Debbie could not manage on her own and David went to live with foster carers. Shaun felt unable to assist because of his detox programme and blamed himself for the family's separation.

As a parent revisits this stage at a later date the potential separation and the heightened expectations become less positive for the child. Each visit becomes more difficult and potentially more damaging as a result.

Maintenance

This is the opportunity that the family have to learn to live together without substances. Often parents will have been through a detox programme or will be on a maintenance prescription of methadone. This is where the child has the chance to learn to be a child and not to have to take on adult responsibilities within the household, as the adults regain control and an appropriate parenting role. Again this can be an exciting time of hopes for the future, and the almost inevitable relapse does not always cloud the family's first experience of this stage.

However, as the family revisit this stage for the second, third or fourth time the experiences can be massively different. Those children interviewed spoke of their constant awareness of the impact of their behaviour on the mood and well being of their parents and the potential for further relapse. Some young people spoke of their parents' difficulties when taking on the caring role of their children after a period of separation. This appeared to be related to their parents' own mixed emotions from the highs of making changes to the lows of not being able to maintain change. This added an extra stress in to the household.

Children at this stage may become aware of the triggers and potential triggers around them which could lead to parental relapse. Each time this stage is revisited the children, who have often become used to taking on high levels of responsibility, have taken on the further responsibility of helping their parents maintain a drug free lifestyle. Disappointment is inevitable as relapse takes place.

Practice Scenario 3

Shona, aged 12, lives with her mother. Her mother is on a methadone prescription. Shona has always been very helpful in the home and has often had to care for herself. On one occasion when her mother relapsed, Shona had been told off in school and the teachers had spoken to her mother. Shona blamed herself for her mother's relapse and has since this time become over anxious about her responsibilities at home and her behaviour in school. She presents as over eager to please with a consistently cheerful disposition which is at odds with the known realities of her own circumstances.

Relapse

It is difficult to talk of the maintenance stage independently of the relapse stage. This is an accepted stage of change and, for those children interviewed, the two stages were viewed together. Relapse is a difficult time for all those involved. For parents there is not only disappointment that they have not succeeded, despite the hard work and effort, but also the feeling that they have let down their children. In some circumstances where there are significant child protection concerns relapse may play a significant part in the planning for the children's future, in some situations leading to the children being placed away from home or not returning home following a period of separation.

For children and young people this stage of change can be particularly traumatic. One common emotion was that of self-blame. Young people would often blame their own behaviour directly for the parent's relapse (Kearney et al., 2005)

Practice Scenario 4

Sarah (aged 9) told staff that her father had shouted at her for not tidying her room, and she should do this to help her mother. The next day her mother had used heroin after a period on methadone. Sarah believed her mother's relapse was her fault.

Kearney (2005) found that older siblings, in particular, took on higher levels of responsibility. Several older children in the group blamed their younger siblings for contributing to the relapse because they couldn't look after themselves well enough or created too much stress at home for their parents.

For some young people their parent's maintenance stage is during a prison sentence, and relapse occurs on release. This is particularly upsetting for young people who have visited parents in prison and witnessed a positive change and the maintenance of a drug-free lifestyle. They have plans and hope for how life will be on their parents release only to be quickly disappointed.

Practice Scenario 5

Jake (10 years) and Leo (6 years) were accommodated with foster parents when their mother was given a custodial sentence for drug related offences. She had been dependent on heroin for two years and there had been concerns about her parenting of Jake and Leo. They had been on the child protection register under the category of neglect prior to their mother's sentence. During her 10 month stay in prison their mother stopped using heroin. She put on weight and looked healthy. She spoke positively with the boys about her release from prison and how things were going to be better. On release she did not attend contact with Jake and Leo but instead met a friend and used heroin. Both boys were extremely disappointed and could not understand their mother's behaviour.

Messages for practice

At each stage of the adult cycle there are many recommendations of appropriate intervention techniques and approaches (Prochaska and DiClemente, 1991; Hamer, 2005). These are helpful and ensure that the worker can apply the most appropriate approach with individuals, dependent on their position on the cycle and their own individual needs.

For the children and young people living through their parents change the interventions and approaches required are less publicised. Most literature takes an adult focus, and does not consider the implications of these adults being parents with parenting responsibilities. It would appear that this adult focus is reflected in the views of those young people who were interviewed. Their expressed dislike of parental change and their struggles to adapt to different stages of the cycle could indicate this.

However, despite the complex emotional turmoil experienced by the young people living through parental change, there appear to be many steps that practitioners could take to alleviate some of the trauma and pain of this difficult process. Unlike the interventions for adults these need not be 'stage' specific but are overarching messages for practice which are not complicated but which already underpin the work we do.

Multi-agency working

As we know multi-agency working is essential to ensuring the well being and safety of children and young people (Murphy, 2004) and when we are working with parental substance misuse it is essential that not only the child care organisations work well together but that multi-agency working crosses the adult-child divide that so often exists (Murphy and Oulds, 2000). This is not without difficulty but is essential if we are to address the process of change from a whole family perspective rather than take a purely child or adult approach.

Only when substance misuse services and children's services communicate and share information in an appropriate way can we hope to put in to place some of the necessary changes required to alleviate the difficulties inherent in the parental change process for children and young people.

Communication

Communication is an essential element in all the work we do. Unfortunately it is often the children and young people we work with who are excluded from the improving lines of communication which exist elsewhere (DfES, 2005). With a bedrock of excellent communication between the service providers, good communication with children and young people could aid in the process of parental change. So often we do not share our understanding of situations with children and young people (Jones, 2003). The young people interviewed (Kearney et al., 2005) clearly indicated a lack of understanding of what their parents may experience whilst undergoing change. This reflects the lack of information given to children and young people in these circumstances.

It is essential that as the parent embarks on the process of change an appropriate worker is identified to explain this process to the child in an age appropriate way. This will enable the child to understand that this is not going to be an easy time and that difficulties are inevitable. For example, if a young person is told that relapse is an inevitable part of recovery, and that this relapse is not dependent on their behaviour, they may not feel the self-blame and responsibility experienced by some of the young people interviewed. If they were able to see it as part of the recovery process, then whilst still disappointed, they may not experience the extreme disappointment expressed by the young people. None of the young people in our sample had been given any explanation of the process of change.

Planning and contingency planning

Good planning is essential in working to safeguard children (Thompson, 2002). When parents are embarking on a process of change, often at the request of an agency, our understanding of the change cycle indicates some of the stages they may go through and how this may impact on them. This can be planned for and appropriate interventions can be provided at each stage (Hamer, 2005).

This planning process must include the children and young people living with parental change if we are to take a whole family approach to change. To plan for the potential disappointments and set backs in advance can ease the process for children and young people. Those young people interviewed (Kearney et al., 2005) identified that separation from parents often as a result of prison sentences was common place. By ensuring that adult criminal justice systems and children's services work together, children can be kept informed and in contact with absent parents.

Conclusion

It is inevitable that government policy and substance misuse services are driven by the desire to get people who misuse substances into treatment. This is a laudable and practical aim. What this chapter begins to challenge is the false assumption that such treatment is an adult-oriented issue only. The people who misuse substances are often embedded within families, with parental and family caring responsibilities. Change and treatment is a whole family issue, a whole family crisis. This chapter strongly advocates the better understanding of adult change as a family and child care process. This understanding then predicts that the change and treatment systems should actively engage children in the change process, in a way that informs and enables them to understand and contribute to it.

References

Alison, L. (2000) What are the Risks to Children of Parental Substance Misuse? In Harbin, F. and Murphy, M. *Substance Misuse and Child Care.* Lyme Regis: Russell House Publishing.

Cleaver, H., Unell, I. and Aldgate, J. (1999) *Children's Needs: Parenting Capacity.* London: HMSO.

DfES (2005) *Common Core of Skills and Knowledge for the Children's Workforce.* London: HMSO.

Elliott, E. and Watson, A. (1998) *Fit to be a Parent: The Needs of Drug Using Parents in Salford and Trafford.* Salford: PHRRC.

Hamer, M. (2005) *Preventing Breakdown.* Lyme Regis: Russell House Publishing.

Harwin, J. and Forrester, D. (2005) *Parental Substance Misuse and Child Welfare.* London: Nuffield.

Hogan, D. and Higgins, L. (2001) *When Parents use Drugs: Key Findings from a Study of Children in the Care of Drug-using Parents.* Dublin: Trinity College.

Jones, D. (2003) *Communicating with Vulnerable Children: A Guide for Practitioners.* London: Gaskell.

Kearney, J. and Taylor, N. (2001) *The Highs and Lows of Family Life: Exploring the Impact of Parental Drug Use in Families.* Salford: IPHRP.

Kearney, J., Harbin, F., Murphy, M., Wheeler, E. and Whittle, J. (2005) *The Highs and Lows of Family Life: Familial Substance Misuse from a Child's Perspective.* Bolton: Bolton ACPC.

Macrory, F. and Harbin, F. (2000) Substance Misuse and Pregnancy. In Harbin, F. and Murphy, M. *Substance Misuse and Child Care.* Lyme Regis: Russell House Publishing.

Mahoney, C. and MacKechnie, S. (2001) *In a Different World.* Liverpool: LHA.

McKeganey, N., Barnard, M. and McIntosh, J. (2002) *Paying the Price for their Parent's Addiction: Meeting the Needs of the Children of Drug Using Parents.* Glasgow: University of Glasgow.

Miller, W. and Rollnick, S. (1991) *Motivational Interviewing: Preparing People to Change Addictive Behaviour.* New York: Guilford.

Murphy, J. et al. (1991) Substance Abuse and Serious Child Mistreatment: Prevalance, Risk and Outcome in a Court Sample. *Child Abuse and Neglect.* 15: 3, 197–211.

Murphy, M. (2004) *Developing Collaborative Relationships in Interagency Child Protection Work.* Lyme Regis: Russell House Publishing.

Murphy, M. and Oulds, G. (2000) Establishing and Developing Co-operative Links Between Substance Misuse and Child Protection Systems. In Harbin, F. and Murphy, M. *Substance Misuse and Child Care.* Lyme Regis: Russell House Publishing.

Prochaska, J. and DiClemente, C. (1982) *Transtheoretical Therapy: Towards a More Integrative Model of Change.* Homewood Ill: Dow Jones/Irwin.

SCODA (1997) *Drug Using Parents: Policy Guidelines for Interagency Working.* London: LGDF.

Thompson, N. (2002) *Building the Future.* Lyme Regis: Russell House Publishing.

Walker, S. and Beckett, C. (2003) *Social Work Assessment and Intervention.* Lyme Regis: Russell House Publishing.

Chapter 7

Developing Whole Family Treatment Services

Fiona Harbin and Michael Murphy

Introduction

Instead of aiming our intervention at adults or children on their own, what value is there in developing services that try to meet the needs of the whole family, from one local base? This chapter will consider how services can best be provided for substance misusing parents and their families through providing flexible and tailored resources aimed at meeting the needs of the whole family.

This chapter brings together three core strands of partnership working. These three strands are particularly relevant to familial substance misuse. The first strand is partnerships between practitioners and parents. The reason why this strand is so important is that the bridge between practitioners and parents who misuse substances is notoriously difficult to achieve (Murphy et al., 1991; Elliott et al., 1998; Elliott and Watson, 2000). The second is the partnership between practitioners and children. Again, in this area, the separate needs of children brought up in substance misusing households are frequently overlooked (Murphy and Harbin, 2000; ACMD, 2003; Kearney et al., 2005). The third strand is partnership between Children's and Adult Services and practitioners. This strand is again one of the most difficult and challenging partnership to attain (Murphy and Oulds, 2000; Kearney et al., 2000; ACDM, 2003). We will see how these strands may come together in the development of new services.

As our main example we will discuss the 'Safer Families Project', a pilot project which ran in Bolton in 2000. Backed by Bolton's Area Child Protection Committee it was funded by the proceeds from a National Conference in 1999 and the publication of *Substance Misuse and Childcare* (Harbin and Murphy, 2000). The project provided more flexible and tailored services for eight families where there were concerns about the levels and nature of parental drug use and the impact this was having on their family life. The families involved included those who had children on Care Orders to those who had children 'in need'. This project was based in a newly opened family centre and offered priority referrals to the existing resources in the area. This included substance treatment services and centre based advice and support, including individual appointments, drop in sessions and children's groups. Three Outreach Workers were employed specifically to provide family support in family homes outside office hours.

Background

Drug use in itself does not amount to poor parenting. Many families have the informal support systems and strategies to manage their drug use and care adequately for their children: 'Most parents who use drugs are 'good enough' parents and do not neglect or abuse their children' (SCODA, 1997: 12). Mountenay (1998: 7) points out that 'many drug users lead perfectly normal lives, some holding down a job and bringing up a family, differing little from their non-drug using peers'. It is also important to note that drug use in itself is not a criterion for inclusion of a child's name on the Child Protection Register or even to state that a child is a 'child in need'.

Whilst research and practice in the field have identified these possible difficulties for families, it cannot be assumed that drug use in itself is impacting on parenting without a thorough assessment of the family situation (Murphy and Harbin, 2003). This should consider the needs of the child, any risk or evidence of significant harm for the child, parenting capacity, how the family copes with drug use, how help can be provided and how willing the parents are to accept and benefit from the help available (SCODA, 1997; Cleaver et al., 1999; Elliott and Watson, 2000). Families may be experiencing many different problems and even if the substance use is addressed, there may not necessarily be an improvement in the overall situation. Mountenay (1998: 36) points out: 'The nature of the link between drug misuse and child abuse is complex, involving factors such as mental illness and poverty'.

In some circumstance, however, parental drug use does lead to problems in the family that impact on the level of care that children receive. It is more likely that drug using families may be socially isolated, spend less time with their children and use inconsistent disciplinary methods (Alison, 2000; Kearney et al., 2005). Although drug use in itself is rarely the only problem experienced by families who are having difficulties, parental substance misuse is recognised as a major contributory factor to child neglect in particular (Forrester, 2000; Harwin and Forrester, 2005).

Dependent drug use can be a time consuming and expensive way of life which may have a two-fold impact on parenting. First there is the immediate impact on the individual's presentation and motor skills, such as drowsiness, inconsistent sleep patterns, poor mental and physical health, mood swings, unpredictability, irritability, lethargy and withdrawal or overdose. All of these could impact on a parent's ability to provide adequate supervision, guidance, boundaries, routine and physical care for their child. Children may be required to take on age inappropriate levels of responsibility not only for themselves but also their siblings and their parents (Mahoney and MacKechnie, 2001; Kearney et al., 2005). Secondly, there can be a more general impact on the lifestyle of the drug user. This may be a result of the offending behaviour associated with drug use, or to fund their drug use. It may include possible prison sentences, association with other dependent drug users and dealers, possible exposure to violent situations, or financial and housing problems. Children may be exposed to risky situations, may have inadequate food, clothing and home environment, there may be periods of separation from their parents which may be distressing and emotionally damaging. The young person may be exposed to drugs and drug use at an early age (SCODA, 1997; Kearney et al., 2005). There is a lack of longitudinal research in to the long-term impact of parental drug misuse on young people, however research into the effects of parental alcohol misuse has identified that children are more at risk of developing mental health problems, attachment problems, behavioural disorders and substance dependency problems (Velleman and Orford, 1999).

Regional and national statistics show an increase in the prevalence of parental drug use impacting on parenting ability. The number of those known to be using drugs is increasing, and within this the gap between the number of male and female drug users is decreasing especially in the 15 to 25 year old age group (Drug Misuse Research Unit, 2002). This disproportionate increase in the number of women users is more likely to have an impact on child care and pregnancy. Mountenay (1998: 7) indicates that '30% of registered addicts are women of child bearing age'. North West drug use figures (2002) indicated that the primary drug used by those requesting treatment is heroin although research in London (Harwin and Forrester, 2005) notes the increasing use, by women, of crack cocaine. Social services figures show an increase in the number of child concern enquiries regarding children living with drug using parents, and almost half of the children who are placed on the Child Protection Register have parents who are dependent drug users (Forrester, 2000). The majority of these children are registered under the category of neglect. The number of children who are presented to the Fostering and Adoption Panel for long-term placements away from their parents have parents who are drug users (Harwin and Forrester, 2005). This reflects research (Curtis and McCullough, 1993; Tracy and Farkas, 1994; Murphy et al., 1991) which shows that drug using parents are likely to reject court ordered services and make service delivery difficult and consequently are likely to have their children removed permanently.

This group of parents face the same barriers as all drug users in accessing services that help them address their drug use. However Elliott et al. (1998: 54) in their study into the needs of drug using parents, found that 'what being (or becoming) a parent did do was to throw some of these barriers into sharp relief'. The barriers for all drug users are identified by Elliott et al. (1998: 3) as: not being able to find time; not identifying their drug use as a problem; anxiety about the knowledge and skills of staff in the treatment agencies; issues of confidentiality and anonymity; the users perceptions of the services available and concern about waiting times for treatment. They explain that female parents also have to face the 'stigma attached to being a drug using parent; fears about losing care and/or custody of the children; and the lack of alternative child care options available'. Services are often seen as predominantly male orientated with little provision for families or child care. There are still widely held views in society that women's drug use is less acceptable than men's. Elliott et al. (1998) quote from the *Observer* newspaper in October 1997, 'No child should be left in the hands of a junkie mother'. With these barriers to overcome services need to be more practically accessible for parents, but also that we need to develop intervention techniques to help parents engage in services. If drug using parents are hard to engage with, it is even more difficult to develop specific services for their children, as the secrecy and stigma of having a drug using parent isolates children and young people (Kearney et al., 2005). With this in mind, when developing specific projects for drug using parents and their children, it is most important that you develop flexible and sympathetic ways of engaging with them, so that two of the three strands of partnership working will be possible.

Setting up a project/making a good beginning

Right at the beginning of the development of a new service it is essential that we address the third strand of partnership working. How do we achieve the full support of the interagency child care system and the interagency (adult) substance system? This strand of partnership working is particularly important when we consider the significant 'gap' between the two systems (Murphy and Oulds, 2000; ACDM, 2003; SCIE, 2003), where the adult system concerns itself with the needs of the adult user, and the child care system concerns itself with the needs of the child and the adult, but only the adult as a parent.

In the Safer Families Project we obtained prior approval from our local ACPC and DAT and then established a multi-agency steering group that brought together representatives from both systems. This group considered how the project should be set up, the nature of the services that could be offered, the aims and objectives and the target group. This group recognised at a very early stage the importance of the provision of a range of flexible services from a venue which would be suitable for whole families. It was agreed that the project should be based in a local area to provide services for one small community rather than aiming to cover a more disparate area.

This steering group met on a monthly basis, with its membership increasingly including those practitioners who were directly involved in working with the families at the project. From these regular meetings and through smaller off shoot meetings, staff were able to identify the necessary resources and services required to set up the project.

Aims and objectives

In any new partnership service or project it is essential to collectively agree the mandate and the goals of the new service before it is set up (Harrison et al., 2003). The aims and objectives of the Bolton project were agreed by the steering group. They are offered here to give an idea of what the family project was trying to achieve:

- To enable children to be free from significant harm or risk of significant harm with their parents.

- To provide a local community based centre for the provision of services for drug using parents and their children.
- To provide multi-agency supportive, therapeutic and assessment services from the same venue.
- To provide accessible, flexible and appropriate services for the families referred.
- To assist parents in meeting their children's needs and to improve their capacity to care.
- To enable children to have a more positive home life.
- To enable children to be more integrated in social activities.
- To promote awareness for the families of the impact of problematic drug use on parenting.
- To ensure that if separation of a child from a family is necessary the reasons, and the timescales for this are understood by family members.
- To provide information for families on other resources available in Bolton.
- To provide a comprehensive exit strategy for each family on completion of the project.
- To provide an anti-discriminatory service.

Identification and engagement with Families

One of the crucial strands of partnership working is the identification and alliance with parents. Substance misusing parents are notoriously difficult to engage with (Murphy, 1991; Elliott et al., 1998). The engagement with parents as clients was essential to the success of the project. It was agreed that services must be provided for families where there were issues of concern. Therefore the project was to provide services for eight families whose children were assessed to be 'in need of support', 'in need of protection' or in the 'looked after' system.

To encourage families to become engaged in the project, a further sessional worker was identified who had personal experience of being a drug using parent who had used local services. This role was developed to help families engage in the project by talking to someone who had had similar difficulties in the past but had been able to overcome them. So at the same time this worker knew the territory well, but also was proof that positive change was possible. This worker was involved in the initial meetings with families and had a further role in other services offered.

We agreed that families who did not immediately attend appointments would not be seen as rejecting the services on offer. Instead care was given to helping families identify what they would find helpful to enable them to better meet the needs of their children, in this way helping services meet the needs of families rather than expecting families to fit into existing resources. Eight families were identified and referred to the project. The predominant drug used by the parents involved was heroin and some parents were on methadone treatment programmes. Poly drug use was believed to be common for most of the parents referred. One parent was maintaining a drug-free lifestyle.

Of the eight families referred, at the time of referral two had children on care orders, one still living with his mother, the other in foster care. Two families had children on the Child Protection Register under the category of neglect, and another family had their unborn baby's name on the Child Protection Register again under the category of neglect. Three of the families had children who were assessed to be in need of support. Generally the concerns about the children related to:

- Lack of provision of basic needs.
- Lack of routine and adequate supervision.
- Exposure to drug use and drugs.
- Ingestion of methadone.
- The taking on of age inappropriate responsibility for themselves, their siblings or their parents.
- Exposure to violence.

Five of the families were two parent families and three were lone parent families. Apart from one drug free couple the other parents were all current drug users. In all at the outset there were thirteen children involved ranging from new born to 13 years. Two babies were born during the course of the project. The families engaged with the project to a greater and lesser degree. This ranged from daily contact seven days a week to no contact for one family (the mother moved to a residential unit and the children went to live with grandparents).

The priority given to engaging families in the project appears to have had some benefit. It is difficult to ascertain what extra levels of engagement were achieved had extra consideration not been given to this area. Many families also indicated that they would have not have attended many of the sessions and meetings had transport not been available.

Staff training, team building and support

In the current climate of integrated teams (DfES, 2003), and the core curriculum (DfES, 2005), the problem of bringing disparate practitioner groups to work together has been widely discussed (Shardlow et al., 2004). Once the aims, objectives and services had been identified those staff most likely to be involved with the project were offered training sessions specifically about the project and what it would entail, with a follow up on factual information on drugs and drug use.

The training events provided were well attended with positive feedback given. They also led to a growing feeling of belonging to a 'team'. However, as with any new services there were still levels of uncertainty about exactly what the project could offer and to whom. As a pilot the number of referrals was limited and this did cause frustration on occasions for staff requiring extra services for families they were working with who were not involved in the project. Some staff reported a growing confidence and expertise in this field having overcome their initial anxieties about the project and working specifically with drug users. Ongoing liaison between the agencies proved to be vital not only in developing the services but in providing support and consultation for all those involved.

Venue

Making a decision about venue is not an easy one. As we know, parents (particularly mothers) can express some reluctance to attend or take children to substance services or social work venues (Elliott and Watson, 2000). Whichever venue is chosen it must be seen as parent and child accessible and friendly. We chose Tonge Moor Family Centre as this centre was seen as child and parent friendly and was conveniently due to open in line with the beginning of the project. The staff at the centre were consulted and re-assured by the offer of support and training. They agreed that the project should be run from their centre and became strong advocates of the 'whole family' way of working. The family centre venue consisted of four converted flats in the centre of a residential area. As a new conversion the centre was well decorated and furnished with the appearance of a family home rather than a local authority venue. The project was able to make full use of the rooms available, namely two family rooms with adjoining kitchens and bathrooms, one with an adjoining play room and a large meeting room with refreshment facilities and an adjoining play room and bathroom. Office facilities were also available. It was negotiated that the project could have priority booking of the rooms and resources. The centre was available to the project in the evenings if required. The centre was always able to accommodate the needs of the project for meetings, family sessions, group work, individual work and administration. Due to the residential location of the centre, and the identification of families in the locality, most families were within easy walking distance. During the course of the project one family moved to live nearer the centre.

The Family Centre staff worked primarily with the families involved with the project. They were able to develop an expertise in working with vulnerable families where the parents were drug users. This was not a new area for the experienced workers at the centre but was an area in which their confidence and knowledge increased dramatically during the course of the project. Staff were extremely flexible in their working hours to supplement the services offered by the outreach workers.

Discovering resources

New services and projects seldom arrive with their own resources in tow. One of the key tasks for any planning group is to discover, access and sometimes create the necessary resources to run the service. With the Safer Families Project it was essential that a complex mixture of services and resources was discovered and provided. The planning group also identified a timescale in which to provide the services.

What services are available in your area? Who are the key players/stakeholders? Could they combine to contribute to a whole family treatment service?

Existing services/extra service provision

The key task with whole family services appears to be to combine current interagency resources, identify the significant gaps that still exist and attempt to develop extra service provision to fill those gaps.

Those parents and children who took part in the project were prioritised for the existing services at the family centre and in the community if they were appropriate for their needs. Many of the families had historical involvement with existing services and it was a priority of the project to provide these services in a way which would be most beneficial to the families expressed needs. Participating agencies had given an undertaking that all staff involved with the project would work in as flexible way as possible within their current role, and that services would be provided from the family centre venue where appropriate. This specifically related to the provision of drug services and treatment, health visiting, midwifery and social work support and assessment. This would obviate the need for families to make journeys to a number of different venues for their appointments.

Three sessional family support workers were employed to provide extra support for families outside the hours of 9.00am to 5.00pm Monday to Friday. This extra support was funded through the money available from the conference, and it was estimated that each of the eight families referred could benefit from up to six hours per week of extra support if required.

A support group for the children involved with the project was available at the family centre. This group was specifically for the children of drug using parents and would look at relevant issues for them, based on an existing Therapeutic Group Work Programme for this group of children. This group was the key to establishing the third strand of partnership, the one that involves practitioners engaging directly with children and young people. The themes that were to arise in the group included; basic drug awareness, self-care and safety issues, self-esteem, identity and bereavement work. All group activity took place in a supportive environment with other children who often had similar experiences. Play and activities were the medium used to help the adults communicate with children and the children to communicate with themselves.

A drop in support group for the parents was available at the family centre. This was planned to run in conjunction with the provision of drug services at the centre. It was planned that the programme of events would be identified by the families involved but could include, amongst other things, relaxation, aromatherapy, welfare rights, health issues and parenting. This combination was key to the strengthening of the first strand of partnership working between parents and practitioners.

Transport would be available for families to attend the family centre for all the services offered. Again, when necessary, this was funded by the money available from the conference but also was accommodated through flexibility of staff involved with the families.

Integrating adult and child care service provision

In setting up the project it had been hoped that most of the existing services provided to families could be provided from the family centre setting. Health visiting and midwifery services were made available from the family centre and three of the families referred were able to take advantage of this service. One family chose not to take advantage of this offer.

It had been planned that the Community Drug Team would be able to offer one afternoon a week to provide appointments for those parents involved in the project. The nature of the project made this a vital element of the services provided. A major barrier that inhibits parents from taking up drug services is their experience of Community Drug Team buildings (Elliott et al., 1998). In particular the lack of child care facilities, the identified risk of the waiting rooms and their difficult locations involving bus journeys with pre-school aged children. By providing a drug service from the family centre many of these barriers to service provision could be removed. Three parents from two families were offered drug services at the family centre, on a fortnightly basis. The feedback from these families was positive and although not all appointments were kept by the parents, one mother who had not engaged in work at the Community Drug Team despite several attempts in the past engaged more successfully with her worker at the centre. Attempts to have a worker available one afternoon or morning per week to see other families involved in the project were unsuccessful due to the difficulties in staffing at the drug team. By the time this became a possibility the pilot project had come to an end.

Unfortunately the lack of this service to one of the families caused them great distress (this had been their initial impetus for becoming involved in the project). They were offered a priority appointment at the Community Drug Team but chose not to become involved with other services provided by the project. Provision was made for those families who had seen their drug worker at the family centre to continue with a drug worker at their GP surgery on the ending of the project.

Parent drop in

The 'drop in' group for parents was to run alongside the service from the Community Drug Team. It was set up to run on a Tuesday afternoon. Despite a suggested programme and the provision of transport and refreshments, no families attended these sessions. Attempts were made to better advertise the service and individual parents made suggestions of what they would find helpful. However, the drop in still failed to attract any of the parents involved.

Feedback from one family suggested that due to the nature of drug use, the taboo that surrounds it and the lifestyle that often accompanies it – drug using parents would find it difficult to attend a group with other drug using parents. Fears related to issues of confidentiality and meeting known acquaintances were also expressed.

After three months our attempts to set up the drop in were ended. It was agreed instead that a non specific drop in group for parents living locally would be more appropriate.

Children's group

Five children attended the Children's Group which ran for the school summer holiday period. This took place one afternoon per week and was run by the project co-ordinator, a member of staff from the family centre and one of the outreach workers. Parents gave permission for their children to attend this group. Previous groups for the children of drug using parents set up prior to the project, had been unsuccessful in engaging children living at home with their parents as parental permission had not been forthcoming.

Due to the differing circumstances of the children who were referred to the project it was difficult to put together a coherent group of similar aged children. On the first session the ages ranged from five years to thirteen years and the activities had to be planned accordingly. The 13 year old and subsequently her 11 year old brother chose not to attend further sessions, stating that they were so much older than some of the other children.

The group was activity based with transport and refreshments provided. All the children were aware of why they were attending but were not required to talk about this if they did not wish to do so. Most chose not to share information about themselves within the group, but often used the car journeys to share information and ask questions.

As previously experienced in groups for children of drug users (Harbin, 2000) where there may be a plethora of family problems, the management of group behaviour was often difficult and at times some of the children needed intensive one to one support. One six year old was unable to manage in the group setting. He became very excited and would exhibit violent behaviour toward the other children and staff. As the group appeared to be distressing for him, and his behaviour was distressing the other group members, he instead spent his time with a member of staff on one to one activities which he appeared to enjoy. He was able during these sessions to explore some of his feelings and thoughts about his home situation.

Family outreach

Three workers were employed specifically to undertake this role to provide extra services for families outside the regular working hours. The services and staff were supervised by the project co-ordinator. Only four of the eight families identified a need for family outreach work. This work involved facilitating family activities, escorting children to school, the provision of transport to child focused activities and vital family appointments and the intensive monitoring of a newborn baby returning home from hospital. The most requested service was for transport to and from appointments and for children to be taken to and from school. One seven year old child who had not attended school for several months was taken to school each morning for several weeks. The service was offered on a decreasing basis with the agreement of the family. The child was able to benefit from the routine and school attendance whilst his mother was able to start making some of the changes necessary for her to take over this role.

One child born two months into the project had older siblings placed for adoption due to the concerns about his parents' ability to care. By offering daily monitoring on discharge from hospital this child was able to go home rather than in to foster care. Daily monitoring, whilst difficult to manage, ensured that the child was cared for but also offered the family regular support and enabled them to build up a relationship with the outreach worker which continued even as the intensity of the support decreased. Despite the high levels of concern at the outset, this child's name was removed from the Child Protection Register within six months and the family are continuing to work closely with the staff at the family centre on a voluntary basis.

The outreach staff were able to provide intensive support and monitoring for one eight year old returning to her parents care from foster care. This high level of involvement enabled a thorough assessment to be undertaken and it was quickly identified when the home environment started to deteriorate. The workers were able to facilitate a quick and appropriate decision for the young person to return to foster care. By regular home visiting at weekends, early mornings and evenings, the workers were often able to see aspects of family life that are not always apparent in the office or arranged day time home visits. Whilst this was helpful in formulating thorough assessments there was also a knock on effect for staff. Working outside office hours could leave staff vulnerable in situations of concern. During the course of the project, staff witnessed the aftermath of violent incidents, abusive situations and hostility from families. Whilst mobile phones were provided along with regular supervision and an on call phone number, it was agreed that the majority of the outreach work would be undertaken by two workers together. This ensured greater staff safety and support, but impacted on the number of hours that could be offered.

It was expected that the provision of the outreach support would be the most expensive aspect of the project. In reality the cost was far less than budgeted for, costing less than £3,000 for the six month period, meaning that there was approximately £7,000 left in the budget on completion of the pilot.

Co-ordination of the project

It was agreed that all the families referred to the project would have an identified key worker (usually a social worker). The key worker and their line manager held case responsibility for the family rather than any staff directly involved in the project. However the services available from the project, the management of the budget and recruitment and supervision of sessional workers was co-ordinated by a specialist senior social worker at the child protection unit, with a remit to work with parental substance misuse. The role of co-ordinator was part time for the duration of the project.

The project initially required intensive involvement from the co-ordinator. Whilst this decreased during the six months the co-ordination of the outreach service, supervision of the staff, the administration, liaison and evaluation were time consuming. As a pilot the project was flexible and as new scenarios arose it was essential that where possible the project provided for the needs of the families involved. The innovative nature of the project and the newness of its remit made its management very time consuming.

Evaluation and outcomes

This section considers the evaluation of the project with reference to the original aims and objectives; the inclusion and engagement in the services of those families referred; the ability of the project to provide the services identified at the outset; the outcomes for and the feedback from the families and staff involved. In other words how did the three strands of partnership develop or fail to develop?

Considering the multiple problems experienced by many of the families involved, we recognised that in certain situations it would not be appropriate for children to remain in, or return to, the care of their parents, even with the extra levels of support that could be offered. In these circumstances it was one of the projects objectives to make separation less harmful to all those involved. We hoped that with the extra services available more thorough and intensive assessments could be undertaken which would aid decision making and the planning of further resources for the families.

Within six months of the pilot project it was possible to set up most of the services which had been planned. However, many of the services were only just becoming established towards the end of the six month period. Drug use is often a chronic problem and even with intensive support it may be unlikely that anything more that the beginning of a process of change can begin in a six month period. However the six months did enable us to identify that as the services were becoming established, some benefits for children and their parents could be seen. The six months were to prove a swift learning process for all involved and staff and families were quickly able to identify which of the proposed services were going to be helpful and which were not.

Feedback from practitioners, parents and children has been generally very favourable. For instance social workers identified that having the extra resources available had allowed speedier and more thorough assessments to be undertaken. Staff had become used to working in a flexible and collaborative way and both family centre staff and other practitioners identified that this has had a knock on effect in other areas of work. Practitioners reported that the project was helpful especially with those families who had appeared to be making no progress (however, this was coupled with some frustration that the services were not available for those families not involved with the project).

Family feedback has been difficult to collect systematically. However, those receiving drug services from the centre spoke very favourably of this, doubting they could have engaged to such an extent if they had been required to attend the Community Drug Team. Frustration was expressed by both families and workers that the Community Drug Team was not able to offer a full service from the family centre as had initially been planned. One family felt that they had been made a false promise and left the project as a result.

The family outreach work was received well by parents and children. Most were pro-active in identifying what would be helpful for their own family. The nature of the work led to families developing positive working relationships with the workers involved.

The children involved in the project were given the opportunity to talk to staff individually or in a group setting about their own experiences. Some of the older ones chose to do so. They showed an awareness of their parents' drug use but often misinformed understanding of the reality of the situation. Again children who were offered outreach support work spoke favourably of their relationship with their outreach worker. Of the 14 children involved only one had to be found substitute care. This move was based on a thorough assessment aided by the intensive involvement of the project and the active cooperation of the child's parents. Two children had their names removed from the Child Protection Register and the majority of the families remain involved with the family centre on a voluntary basis.

Conclusion

This chapter has been concerned with the possibility of better meeting child and family needs by offering a whole family treatment service. By attempting to tie the three strands of partnership working together, whole family treatment services seems to create a way of working that can intervene in a powerful way into some families lives. By attempting to engage children, parents and substance and child care staff in one location, the treatment needs of all the family can be met in a more comprehensive and interlocking way. Some readers may believe that it was the intensity of the services that were offered that made the difference. But we would contend that this group of families are resource and labour intensive at all times. It was the tying together of the three strands of partnership that seems to have made the difference (it was also significant that the project was far less expensive than expected).

In our current climate of organisational change, children's services are subject to greater integration and adult mental health and substance services have moved into their own mental health trusts. These change processes may make whole family provision around substance problems more difficult to achieve, yet more essential if we are better to meet the needs of this group of parents and children.

This chapter ends on a cautionary note. Although the project was judged to have been very successful, the rolling out of this pilot in the rest of the borough proved to be much more difficult than originally expected. Because the original reticulists (Murphy, 1996) moved on to other employment and because of the complexity of change processes in both children's and adult sectors, the rolling out of the whole family approach has undergone significant organisational delays.

References

Advisory Committee on the Misuse of Drugs (2003) *Hidden Harm*. London: HMSO.

Alison, L. (2000) *What are the Risks to Children of Parental Substance Misuse?* In Harbin, F. and Murphy, M. (2000) *Substance Misuse and Child Care*. Lyme Regis: Russell House Publishing.

Cleaver, H., Unell, I. and Aldgate, J. (1999) *Children's Needs: Parenting Capacity*. London: HMSO.

Curtis, P. and McCullough, C. (1993) The Impact of Alcohol and Other Drugs on the Child Welfare System. *Child Welfare*. 72, 533–42.

DfES (2003) *Every Child Matters*. London: HMSO.

DfES (2005) *Common Core of Skills and Knowledge for the Children's Workforce*. London: HMSO.

Drug Misuse Research Unit (2002). *Greater Manchester Drug Misuse Database Report*. University of Manchester.

Elliot, E. and Watson, A. (2000) *Responsible Carers, Problem Drug-Takers, or Both?* In Harbin, F. and Murphy, M. (Eds.) *Substance Misuse and Child Care*. Lyme Regis: Russell House Publishing.

Elliot, E., Watson, A.J., Harries, U., Landes, R., and Siddall, J. (1998) *Fit to be a Parent: The Needs of Drug Using Parents in Salford and Trafford*. Salford: PHRRC Research Report No. 8.

Forrester, D. (2000) Parental Substance Misuse and Child Protection in a British Sample. *Child Abuse Review*. 19: 235–46.

Harbin, F. and Murphy, M. (Eds.) (2000) *Substance Misuse and Childcare: How to Understand, Assist, and Intervene When Drugs Affect Parenting*. Lyme Regis: Russell House Publishing.

Harrison, R., Mann, G., Murphy, M., Taylor, A. and Thompson, N. (2003) *Partnership Made Painless: A Joined up Guide to Working Together*. Lyme Regis: Russell House Publishing.

Harwin, J. and Forrester, D. (2005) *A Study of Social Work With Families in Which Parents Misuse Drugs or Alcohol*. London: Nuffield Foundation.

Kearney, J. and Taylor, N. (2001) *The Highs and Lows of Family Life Research Report*. Salford: University of Salford.

Kearney, J., Harbin, F., Murphy, M., Wheeler, E. and Whittle, J. (2005) *The Highs and Lows of Family Life: Familial Substance Misuse From a Child's Perspective*. Bolton: Bolton ACPC.

Kearney, P., Lenin, E. and Rosen, G. (2000) *Alcohol, Drug and Mental Health Problems: Working With Families.* London: NISW.

Mahoney, C. and MacKechnie, S. (2001) *In a Different World: Parental Drug and Alcohol Use: A Consultation Into its Effects on Children and Families in Liverpool.* Liverpool: LHA.

Mountenay, J. (1999) *Drugs, Pregnancy and Child Care: A Guide for Professionals.* London: ISDD.

Murphy, J.M., Jellinek, M., Quinn, D., Smith, G., Poitrast, F. and Goshko, M. (1991) Substance Abuse and Serious Child Mistreatment: Prevalence, Risk and Outcome in a Court Sample. *Child Abuse and Neglect.* 15: 3, 197–211.

Murphy, M. (1996) *The Child Protection Unit.* Aldershot: Ashgate.

Murphy, M. (2004) *Developing Collaborative Relationships in Interagency Child Protection Work.* Lyme Regis: Russell House Publishing.

Murphy, M. and Harbin, F. (2000) *Background and Current Context of Substance Misuse and Child Care.* In Harbin, F. and Murphy, M. (Eds.) *Substance Misuse and Child Care.* Lyme Regis: Russell House Publishing.

Murphy, M. and Harbin, F. (2003) The Assessment of Parental Substance Misuse and its Impact on Childcare. In Calder, M. and Hackett, S. (Eds.) *Assessment in Childcare: Using and Developing Frameworks for Practice.* Lyme Regis: Russell House Publishing.

Murphy, M. and Oulds, G. (2000) *Establishing and Developing Cooperative Links Between Substance Misuse and Child Protection Systems.* In Harbin, F. and Murphy, M. (Eds.) *Substance Misuse and Child Care.* Lyme Regis: Russell House Publishing.

SCODA (1997) *Drug Using Parents: Policy Guidelines for Interagency Working.* London: LGA Publications.

Shardlow, S., Davis, C., Johnson, M., Long, T., Murphy, M. and Race, D. (2004) *Education and Training for Interagency Working: New Standards.* University of Salford.

Social Care Institute for Excellence (2004) Parenting Capacity and Substance Misuse. Research Briefing No. 6. London: SCIE.

Tracy, E.M. and Farkas, K.J. (1994) Preparing Practitioners for Child Welfare Practice with Substance-abusing Families. *Child Welfare,* 73: 57–68.

Velleman, R. and Orford, J. (1999) *Risk and Resilience: Adults Who Were the Children of Problem Drinkers.* London: Harwood Academic.

Chapter 8

Where it all Begins: Growing Up and the Helping Relationship

Phil Harris

Introduction

Relationships make us human. Studies into the effects of prolonged isolation on segregated prisoners, Antarctic explorers, sub-mariners or astronauts demonstrate the centrality of relationship to human behaviour. These groups all experience cognitive impairment, depression, anxiety, rages, hostility, amotivation and even a loss of identity itself through protracted separation. We define, and are defined by, the webs of relationships we forge. They are the very medium in which we live. So dominant are the attachments, allegiances and associations that we form, and so damaging the separations and exclusions we experience, some theorists suggest that individualistic psychology as a discreet discipline is simply not possible (Erikson, 1994). Only a social psychology can capture the interplay that shapes us. The fact that we live in a world of relations is reflected in the epidemiology of child and adolescent problems. The development of disorders correlates with relationship breakdowns within the family, peer or institutions that young people occupy. This is particularly salient for children reared in high consuming households, where the risk of developing drug and alcohol problems, alongside a host of associated disorders, is considerable (Dadds and McAloon, 2002). Similarly, outcome research consistently identifies helping relationships as significant in all therapeutic outcomes. Lambert's (1992) analysis of treatment suggests 30 per cent of outcomes are driven purely by the relationship between the helper and the helped. Relationship factors with young people may be even more significant. Adult models of counselling are too intellectually demanding for young people, who may not have achieved the cognitive maturity to self-monitor, or emotional literacy to articulate complex and contradictory feelings in ways these interventions demand (Roth and Fonagy, 1996). The relationship may be the only medium we have in working with young people but even this demands a caveat: because what a relationship means to adults and young people is very different. As such, this chapter will explore how we can embrace this difference and use relationship factors alone to produce powerful outcomes with young people.

Adolescence: remember when?

A key component of any helping relationship is that of 'empathy', that is, to be able to see the world as the client sees it. The adult practitioner working with a young person can easily forget they are looking back at this young person's life from a more developmentally sophisticated position. Their concerns and aspirations are not the same as the young person's, and their seasoned experience of dealing with stresses and tribulations far outweighs their client's. To the practitioner, solutions can appear obvious or problems insignificant. A paternalistic desire to make the young person's world okay combined with the apparent incompetence of youth to recognise, let alone remedy the problem, can entice the practitioner to take up the reigns of their client's life and steer them in the right direction. And, with all the good intentions in the world, completely alienate the individual they sought to help. Without recognising the intrinsic difference between adult and adolescent world views, we are, as Kegan (1994) said, on one side of the river, shouting ever louder for young people to cross, in a foreign language.

Young people occupy a very different developmental niche, where goals, values and even the concept of relationships take very different forms. Relationships serve very different functions. The young person is embedded in polar axis of relationships between peers and adults. The peer group itself is a platform to enable young people to explore both the external world around them, in terms of guided and group-limiting risk taking activities; as well the internal world in rehearsing relationships of intimacy, trust, loyalty and belonging. Young people are novice in the relationships they select for themselves, and in maintaining the mutual consideration relationships demand. The best friend, the gang, the rapid fire romances all provide rehearsals for our capacity to relate to others in later life. The values of authenticity, genuineness and loyalty take on enormous significance as they test out trusting others with the intimacy of their thoughts and feelings for the first time. As the young person's identity is still fledgling at this juncture, peer groups of identification serve to shore up the deficits in the identity that is forming. At a cognitive level, the development of values depends on the capacity of inference.

Young people, who read their life as a sequence of events, slowly learn to reach beyond the surface activity and grasp what drives events in their life. This process takes time to formulate. In the interim, belonging to a peer group is to align themselves to a set of shared or self-supporting group values that are a significant identity prop for them. These values are often sourced in popular cultures and fashions. Hence, young people do not seek out adult role models, but identify with over-inflated adolescent figures like pop idols, actors and footballers, who are essentially older versions of themselves that caricature key values and lifestyles. Our perennial concerns about the music young people listen to is not a question of taste but one of the ethics and lifestyles that adolescents align their identity with. Like the peer group, the chosen egocentric and hedonistic figures of popular culture serve as an interim bridge, as the young person re-locates their values away from the family towards their own selves.

For adolescents, the peer group is a badge of office where identify is inferred by the trappings of group identity, explored in the collective safety of watchful others and cemented in their obligations to significant others. Self-belief is relatively low at this stage of development, and young people have little or no control over the world they are embedded in. A young person does not feel disempowered though, provided they have 'equal' power and personal freedom as their peers. The group thus serves as a barometer of their shift from dependence to independence, where deficiencies are assessed through comparison and redressed by pressuring adults to allow them to keep up with the freedoms of their peers.

Great divides

Young people are thus leaving home in degrees. From an early age young people police a very clear divide between home and public life. Whilst they will let public life come into home, they will not let their home become an agenda item for the peer group. Young people in care have no private retreat from public life. And any practitioner who wishes to reach beyond the presenting concerns into their family life is expecting the young person to breach a deep cultural code of silence. Especially when the young person has an intuition that their home life might single them out as different.

Young people can perceive adults as a restraining force on their exploration and independence. The relationships that they have with adults are limited to formal structures where power is decreed by role rather than by mutual negotiation. Parents and teachers are locked into the formal power structures of family and school. They provide the dual function of both holding young people, as well as providing a framework to kick against. These roles should serve as a brake on young peoples' desire for freedom beyond their competence to manage. Whilst this may be important in the early to mid-teen years, these restraining forces can become the ground of increasing conflicts as the young person reaches late adolescence. These social frameworks that held and restrained must let go timely, leaving the young person adequately prepared to begin the construction of their own framework of living. The transition into adulthood is to leave these surrogate institutions and define one's own, in the form of their own relationships, family, home, work and leisure. It is the clash of these emerging values with peer and family norms that will enable the young person to grow through these structures. The resultant conflict drives them to separate from structures that are not letting them go timely.

For young people growing in high consuming families these careful cultural balances and counter-balances of development can be skewed. The parents may model only dysfunctional relationships, exert little parental control and allow their wards too much freedom, removing the brake from total emersion in an unchecked peer group. High availability of substances may expose young people to use at an early age, without witnessing any informal regulation or recognition of unacceptable thresholds of consumption. The result is often exclusion from the mainstream social institutions where many broader rehearsals for life are enacted. Alternatively, drug using parents who place high support needs on their children equally deny them involvement in these broader social institutions of peers and school. Excessive responsibility for parents smothers the practice and rehearsal necessary for their own development. The net result is the same for those young people so estranged from family, or so embedded in them that they become dislocated from peers: developmental delay.

Relationships of a different order

This places the worker with young people in a unique position. Between the horizontal relationships to peers, and the vertical relationships with adults, those working with young people occupy new ground. The power and the difficulty in effective working with young people reside not merely in the abatement of specific problems; but in initiating a major re-orientation in how young people experience relationships. The worker represents the first adult relationship of equality that this young person may have experienced. And mastering relationships with adults as peers is what will shape their future life. As such, the helping relationship with dislocated young people replaces deficits and can provide preparedness for a new way of being in the world.

The novelty of the worker-young person encounter creates initial difficulties in the working relationship. Young people expect a certain kind of relationship with adults of restraint. They will be expecting the worker to be as the teacher or parent and will fortify themselves against being directed once again to some end not clear to them but desired by the adult. This may be compounded by the young person having had a great deal of experience of professionals, many of which are not constructive. The highly 'treated' young person will soon begin testing our liberal values to see if we are anything more than the apes of our ideals. Understanding this is important because young people are especially prone to reactance (Brehm and Brehm, 1981).

When they sense personal threat or loss of personal freedom they will formulate a contradictory opinion, even if the suggestions are in their own interest. And the low self-belief of young people means they are easily threatened. Combined with this is the fact that we do not have a preset menu of opinions on everything. We learn our opinions as we speak them. Thus, if we enter into a relationship with young people selling an angle, young people will not only contradict it but will justify the contradiction in ways which cement their current behaviour. This demands that we enter into relationships with young people with an *open mindedness* rather than *change-mindedness*.

Collaborative encounters

Whilst they may have been referred and detailed case notes might exist on the young person, often they are diagnosis from an adult perspective. Furthermore, the home and public divide often means that so many parental, peer or school assessments rarely corroborate each other anyway as young people's behaviour is so very situational (Roth and Fonagy, 1996). Asking the young person why they think they have been referred to you and what their own concerns are can allow them space to put their own view forward and be respected. They can tell their story of the presenting problems from their own perspective and allow them their slant on events, even if this is driven by their injustice of the referral.

Once the story is told, one question which I find useful to ask is 'How have you come to explain all this to yourself?' This reveals a great deal of insight into how the young person makes sense of the world. The kind of answer they offer demonstrates their cognitive maturity as to whether they can offer psychological explanations of others and their own behaviour; how well they recognise or manage contradictory feelings; their readiness to engage in change; and more importantly offers considerable insight into possible helpful approaches. For example, one young person once answered this question by expressing how totally unbearable revisiting an abusive childhood was for him, suggesting that a solution orientated approach would be more helpful. Whilst another young person wondered deeply about their relationship with an inconsistent and explosive mother suggesting a more retrospective approach would build on his current understanding. In this way we can get beside the young person's understanding and build upon it rather than against it.

Foremost it is important to understand that problems or maladaptive behaviours mean something to the young person. They often serve some useful function for them.

Whilst young people are not choosing to have problems, once difficulties occur they can develop around them and use the problem as a means of dealing with demands of life in light of skills deficits. Coming in suggesting, or even hinting at, change will send them deeper into defending the value of problems or inability to change. So initial conversations should not be problem focused but instead aim to understand the behaviour as it occurs to the young person. Recognising the value and function of the behaviour first defies the young person expectations of the worker, allows them to voice their own concerns and tends to play on a reverse psychology of the rules of reactance. It does not take long for a young drug user, swelled with the pride of their knowledge of drugs to then say, 'Yes, but drugs are bad for you, aren't they . . .?'

Accepting, not necessarily agreeing with, the reality that the young person's behaviours have positive and negative functions will open the dialogue. This is especially useful if the young person is deliberately stone walling you. Their angry silence is a refusal to let you into their private thoughts and should be respected. I heard one therapist's account of working with such young people, who continually appeared for sessions but would say nothing. Their first utterance was invariably 'Will you stop staring at me.' Instead, talking about context of wider issues may draw them out, allow them to express expertness and thus reside in a comfort zone of confidence.

During the initial stages it is important to be watchful of deploying too many counselling 'techniques.' Young people's preoccupation with genuineness and authenticity makes them suspicious of being 'worked.' They can smell a counselling technique like a shark detects a drop of blood. Any hint of contrivance may be experienced as being 'steered' towards a concern and will generate a reactance where they are adamant not to play the game, or trap, that you are setting. Counselling techniques should thus be used sparingly with young people until the relationship is well established. Working with young people is a delicate act of timing: knowing when to be the resourceful friend and when to be the practitioner. The relationship and issues should be allowed to unravel as naturally as possible. This also serves to model a directness and honesty necessary for healthier, open relationships. Where the young person becomes stuck on an issue, the right technique is very useful. But it must be delivered without affect and relate to the young person's immediate experience as closely as possible. The concrete thinking of young people means that they may not relate abstract ideas to themselves.

The unstated contract

To be cautious with techniques is not to suggest that managing relationships in therapy is easy, innate or without craft and self-awareness. All too often a practitioner's incantation that the work is all about the relationship is a defence of ignorance rather than a description of effective practice. It begs the question of what is helpful about the relationship and how do we know we are providing it? The mechanics of relationships are well researched and are universally accepted as integral to producing good outcomes. Technique can be understood as merely maximising the relationship, keeping the rapport flowing by resolving, illuminating or identifying key obstacles and opportunities as the relationship unfolds. Bordin's (1979) little known but seminal paper first outlined the core ingredients of successful relationships in the establishment of the therapeutic alliance. He identified three core ingredients, the establishment of goals; the agreement of tasks; and the mutual bond between the helper and the helped. It is important to understand these three concepts, and some of the common pitfalls in practice with young people.

The goal is the defining reason that the helper and the helped come together. It can be assumed that this goal will hinge on some need for change in the young person's life. Ultimately, despite the diversity of possible disorders that could be encountered, this change is usually a desire the client has to move closer to an ideal they have of themselves, or someone has of them, which feels unobtainable in the normal course of their life. The orientation of the therapy and the organisational aims of the service provider define the scope for the helper to collaborate on achieving these goals. For example, some behavioural therapies may set very specific goals to address key behaviours, whilst developmental or existential interventions may look at what lies beneath a multitude of symptomatic behaviour and thus addresses global change. At other times the wants of the client may simply fall outside the range of service provision being offered. Certainly the goal of the helper is nearly always to see the young person changed for the better. It makes our life meaningful to think we have done some good for this person. This can mean that the failure of our clients attacks our personal goals and can lead to resentment or frustration in our aspirations not being realised.

The establishment of goals has evolved with some refinement. As deShazer (cf. Hoyt, 1994) stated 'If the therapist's goals and the client's goals are different, the therapist is wrong'. This marks a new ethos in counselling away from the goal setting agendas of the 'expert' towards collaborating with the wants of the client. We are all cursed and blessed to define the nature of own lives and these wants cannot be supplanted by the aspirations of others. For young people, having to make life course defining decisions about which path they should take, this is a particularly sensitive time. Though, we should be careful not to confuse motivation with goals. Young people are always motivated to some end, they may just not be motivated for what we are offering. Young people's goals vary from the humble to extravagant. To adults they may represent unrealistic projections of fantasy futures. But, like their behaviours, we must recognise that these goals mean something to the young person that cannot be dismissed, even if they feel unobtainable. Asking the young person what they would like to achieve invites their opinion and their answers need to be respected as meaningful. We should not limit young people to wanting only the things that we think are right for them. For the truly fantastical answers, the follow up question of 'And what would you find so good about that?', can unearth more everyday concerns that are obtainable and intrinsically important to this young person. To be 'a professional footballer' may actually be about recognition, status and acceptance. To 'live on my own' may well represent freedom, choices and the possibility of greater autonomy. These are areas which can be worked on in the helping relationship relatively easily as goals for the young person. Of course, we should be careful not to tread on a young person's dreams. Many socially excluded young people do go on to achieve great things. The expectations of adults around socially excluded young people can dampen their expectations of themselves. In a classic experiment where teachers were told which children were 'gifted' and which were 'under achievers,' a divide in attainment soon opened up in these groups, even though they were in reality identical (Tauber, 1997).

The journey to oneself

Goals can be considered as ideals which must be turned from intention into action. The way we achieve goals demands we engage in certain active physical tasks. The nature of these tasks is once again dependant on the orientation of the treatment model and the organisational provision, be it counselling, education or outward bounds. The fulfilment of the tasks demands that young people are open to engagement and honesty in reflecting on the processes that they invoke, be it emotional awareness, confidence building or self-monitoring of behaviour. Again, the greater the closeness of fit between the tasks and the goals of the client the better the compliance will be. This is especially true for young people, who may not be able to translate activities in one area, for example achievement in climbing a mountain, with addressing a goal in another area, increasing self-confidence to overcome an addiction.

Whilst we over-assess and over-refer many young people, little consideration is given to the young person's perspective of such handing over. Young people's low self-belief means that they are often deeply concerned about exposing incompetence and so are likely to 'act out' or 'walk out' on activities that they experience as formidable. Furthermore, in later adolescence young people find it difficult to enter into pre-formed peer groups and do not engage easily in these situations. In the absence of any experience of the service being offered, they will build positive or negative expectations that may hype or shun the activity before it has even begun. Checking out what their expectations are, and explaining how the services are designed to help their specific problem is important in clarifying the referral to the young person and helping them evaluate its usefulness. Visiting possible referral services with young people, allowing them to get an experience of them without any obligation to engage will often limit the reactance which so often sabotages referral attempts.

The bond can be considered as the mutual respect which exists between the young person and the worker. This can include the Rogerian qualities of empathy, positive regard and congruence that need to be reciprocated. If the young person and the practitioner cannot find mutual points of respect then the relationship will struggle.

As Erikson (1995) warned, we should not mistake the symptoms for the child, and even if it is only the bloody-minded defiance of our wards to preserve their self-autonomy at any cost, we can still value and admire their tenacity. Certainly, young women are more relationship orientated. In groups they will sacrifice activities to preserve relationship harmony and so may find the trusting bond important. Young men resolve difficulties only to pursue activities and so may be less inclined to open up and more inclined to attain the demands of the task. This suggests that the bonds between the helper and the helped may be multi-faceted, in that young people may be prepared to share information on various aspects of themselves to varying degrees to the same person.

The broken alliance

It is essential to establish the alliance with young people in any setting, with even the efficacy of prescribed psychiatric drugs being largely determined by the relationships they are administered in (Krupnick et al., 1996). In reality, whilst these three core aspects are separated out they do inform each other. With this strong bond, the young person is more likely to follow through on tasks. Likewise, if the tasks appear helpful, this will deepen the bond. This collaborative interplay is important in fostering change in any area as recent research highlights that motivation is not a character trait. Instead it emerges in relationships when young people are achieving goals important to them in ways they can manage in an atmosphere of trust and respect (Miller and Rollnick, 2002). Compliance can only be achieved through this means. This puts a greater emphasis on the worker as a key ingredient in treatment rather than the outcome being the sole preserve of the client. The more we impose upon the client, the more they resist (Patterson and Forgatch, 1985). As such, monitoring the relationship is important. If there is tension between the practitioner and the young person, it is better to focus on this and restore the alliance than to continue addressing wider issues.

Conflicts and tensions are a part of relationships and facets of living that young people must learn to manage like any other. Dealing with conflicts openly and accepting responsibility for mistakes non-defensively is vital in modelling relationship conflicts with young people. I have only known young people respond positively to me acknowledging an error on my part. And more importantly it fosters reciprocation. When more complex difficulties arise, an understanding of the relationship dynamics may assist us in bypassing the impasse with relative ease, without recourse to complex interventions and can indeed deepen the bond between the practitioner and the young person.

Relational shifts

Certainly, as the relationship unfolds we are to expect difficulties. Working with very challenging young people, with undeveloped social skills, experiencing complex problems can leave the practitioner at a loss of how to deal with content of the session and the process of helping. However, many obstacles may be overcome simply by changing the perspective on the relationship. Let us consider what is happening when the worker and the young person come together. Essentially we have an experienced, trained professional adult and a young person disrupted within an adolescent developmental niche, meeting each other in an encounter where neither can fully understand what is happening. There is an aspect both understand; an aspect of internal drives and contexts that only the client understands; an aspect of later life, clinical experience and personal context only the helper knows; and finally, an area which neither understand. Shifting between these four areas will often move 'stuck' encounters and open up new and powerful areas of concern.

The area of common agreement is the shared ground of the discussion between the practitioner and the young person. These are the ground rules shared, issues raised, questions asked and answered. Our counselling training primarily focuses on shared ground and how we construct the rapport that unfolds between the helper and the helped. And this is the area which may meet with a multitude of tensions. Classic problems such as identifying core issues, where to go next, conflicts in opinion, resistance towards moving towards a goal or accepting tasks emerge here. Where obstacles do arise, debating them makes problems more protracted, demoralising both individuals and erodes trust.

When encountering problems in the shared ground we can shift to one of the other perspectives. For example, the practitioner is hearing what the client is saying, but they are also watching the client. Before them is a kind of dance, with the client signalling a rich array of messages. Besides what they disclose, they have styles, patterns and assumptions loading how they deliver the message. Isolating the client in action and noticing what they are doing can give a deep insight into the problem.

Scenario 1

I was working with a young person with an anxiety disorder who was becoming increasingly agitated about not receiving a call from his estranged father that he missed deeply. He unleashed a flood of questions as to why his father had not called. It would be impossible to address every question in the shared ground and any discussion would have been highly speculative. Instead I observed. What he appeared to be doing was trying to solve this issue as if it were a puzzle, and that finding an answer would protect him from something fearful. In the client's language, I shared this observation and asked what might the answer do for him? This question stopped the client in the tracks of his rushing thoughts and calmed him greatly. It opened up new shared ground, of coming to terms with his father's inability to fully understand him and how the constant disappointments had impacted his emotional state. Understanding this allowed him to begin to fortify an increased sense of independence, minimising the effect on his mental health.

Conversely, the client is watching our dance of signals and messages too. As we have seen, the relationship is mutually constructed and we are bringing much to the encounter. The client is always collaborating with our attempts to support them, telling us what we are getting right and what we are getting wrong. They may do this indirectly through disengagement or directly in no uncertain terms. We are not always sensitive to developing an ear for this, but very often resistance in the client is important feedback to the practitioner that they are doing something wrong. Listening to this feedback from the client is very important and, I suspect, is actually how practitioners sub-consciously learn their craft.

Scenario 2

Whilst waiting to see a client in the TV room of a psychiatric hospital, I observed an interesting discussion between a nurse and a depressed young woman, obviously experiencing anorexia. The young woman had been watching television quietly when the female nurse approached wanting to discuss an issue with her. The young woman said she did not want to discuss the issue with this nurse as she did not listen to her. The nurse insisted that she did listen. The young woman insisted she did not. The nurse insisted that she did, the young woman increasing insisted that she did not. This tennis match of refutation soon escalated in emotional intensity leaving the young woman screaming in frustration, orderlies were called and the nurse disengaged, no doubt ascribing the cause of the patient's distress to her illness rather than this particular interaction. If at any point had this nurse listened to the feedback from the young woman, and openly explored what she was not hearing, the incident would not have happened. The relationship would have moved forward and the nurse would have learned something valuable about her practice. We should be careful not to protect our evolving competence by forcing our clients to accept themselves as incompetent.

The fourth perspective that we can take is the bird's eye view that neither person grasps. When a young person either refuses to engage, is cynical, leaves all the talking up to the practitioner or reacts powerfully to innocuous events, this may be sourced in motives neither person is fully aware of. Trying to step out of this situation and look at it from a more detached perspective can often move the relationship forward. Imagine if you like, that you were watching these two people on a video with no sound. Asking what are these two people are both doing illuminates where the tensions lie.

Scenario 3

A young person was facing exclusion from school after throwing a chair out of a closed window during a lesson. The teacher had made a negative remark and the reaction was swift and dramatic. The shared ground was dominated by the young person's insistence that the teacher was an arsehole and they did not consider that they themselves had any issue. Sitting back I thought about what we were doing. I said it felt as though I was trying to convince them of something they could not recognise, that whilst the teacher was wrong, his reaction to this was very powerful. I asked if anything like that had ever happened to him before? What emerged was the stigma of his dyslexia, how his parents' low expectations and persecutions had made him feel stupid. It had eroded his confidence in himself and I could sense a great deal of shame. The teacher's comment had been to call him 'an idiot' for being mildly disruptive. It touched a much deeper fracture line of public shame in him and exposed his inadequacy. This young person made wider connections, and became less threatened by criticism.

Young people may react very powerfully at times. But they do not react for no reason, just for ones which often elude both the young person and the practitioner. Adopting this outside perspective liberates us from being stuck 'inside' the problem and allows us to consider the 'nature' of the problem itself.

The emperor's new self-worth

Whilst the therapeutic alliance appears to place total emphasis on realising the wants of the client, this is not the whole picture. This collaborative orientation of relationships of equality with young people places a very high demand on them. The attainment of goals depends on the young person's performance in constructing the outcomes. The under-parented have not operated within containing frameworks whilst for our over-parented, self-regulation has been governed by others, not their own capacity. Negotiation of the relationship of equality is thus expecting the under-parented to stop over-shooting in their behaviour whilst the over-parented must stop under-shooting. This demands moving towards a self-regulatory norm which they may not yet comprehend but must learn to infer. Supporting young people to achieve a new norm of behaviour is challenging, demanding and difficult. With limited, if any, prior experience, these young people have little else to operate on other than our guided mastery and their own expectations. As a result they will often continue to over or under-shoot in initial change attempts. Young people tend to learn through self-correctional processes. They attempt a change task from a position of naiveté and must evaluate performance in order to hone it. This is similar to the process of learning to play a video game, where they get stuck on one of the digital challenges. Here they must generate a hypothesis of how to overcome the difficulty, try it out, evaluate and build on what appears promising and discard what does not. In this way they foster self-belief through direct mastery. And like the video game it demands engagement, perseverance and resolve to overcome initial disappointments whilst trusting that there is a solution. The challenge for the helping relationship is to assist in the learning process by building young people's ability for self-reflection on experience.

One mistake we commonly make in this is the over-emphasis of two fashionable concepts. The first is the perennial obsession with consequences. Young people do not necessarily relate to this concept for one specific reason. Lack of broader experience means that young people enter into situations or activities with expectations, that if I do 'X' then 'Y' follows. The events or behaviours are enacted and then these must be interpreted by young people. They then interpret the events *according to their expectations*. The more positive the expectations they hold, the more problematic the behaviour. This means that anything that does not conform to their expectations is discounted. So, asking a young person about the consequences of their self-harming, alcohol use or aggression will only elicit the positive consequences that they anticipate. They see not the problem but the expectations. As such, it is the expectation that needs to be addressed by exploring what does not conform. For example, a young drinker may have positive expectations of alcohol which do not feature vividly in the description of their drinking events, reflecting this back can provoke a re-evaluation of what they think this behaviour is doing for them.

The second preoccupation of adults for working with young people is the notion of raising low self-esteem. Many young peoples' problems centre on artificially high self-esteem, which may minimise their sense of threat or over-estimate their ability to cope with problems. These 'confident incompetents' may figure highly in anti-social behaviour groups. As a result, research into raising self-esteem demonstrates negative and not positive outcomes for young people (Elliott, 2002). It is important to recognise that self-esteem is a product of behaviour not a driver of it. A young offender on a successful crime spree may derive much self-esteem from this behaviour. It is a question of whether they have the self-belief that they can achieve this via any other means which is the issue. Self-belief is the greatest predictor of educational and therapeutic achievement (Schwarzer, 1992).

Soothing self-esteem may be damaging in young people's learning because it affects the self-correctional process. When a young person engages in behaviours with a positive expectancy, and they encounter negative social punishments, it creates the dis-conforming data that forces them to re-evaluate overtly positive expectations (Goldman et al., 1993). For example, one young person I worked with presented one day looking deflated. That weekend he had gone to a night club with friends. Here he met a young woman he was attracted to and they got on well. However, the large volume of alcohol he consumed meant he threw up over her shoes, so ending the blossoming relationship abruptly. Here was an opportunity to contrast his expectations of alcohol with negative social realities and allow him to consider what alcohol was actually doing for him. The blow to his self-esteem forced him to re-evaluate overtly positive expectations about drinking, reducing his consumption. As such, negative social cues or damage to other prized goals, is a natural instigator of self-correctional processes in young people. It is the discomfort of negative emotional states that prompts change, and so artificially mollifying negative emotions such as low self-esteem, anxiety about current behaviour or shame may remove the impetus for change. Young people who are unrehearsed in considering their behaviour, or those in family-peer groups where negative social realities are normalised, may need their attention alerted to the contrasts of positive expectancies and negative realities to mediate behaviours.

Institute of self-correction

The role of self-correction plays a wider part in development. Young people are developing very quickly, and what is being developed are new internal powers that they have little skill in managing. For example, a three year old may develop the power to walk and talk without thinking about it. And they walk and talk all over the place. At the age of eleven young people gain the power of empathy, and can see themselves as others see them. The intensity of the new self-gaze can overwhelm them and reduce the once ebullient child into a withdrawn and defensive teenager. At puberty an adolescent may over sexualise their appearance. Learning how to manage these newly emerging aspects of self is a struggle and young people may be as clumsy here as they are with controlling the rapid growth of their physical bodies.

Responsibility for these powers does not emerge internally but are policed through the culture they are embedded in. For so many socially excluded young people, the lack of restraining forces which direct the deployment of these powers, or the dominance of parental influence which removes any opportunity for the expressions of the powers, means these skills must be learned in other forums. The fatiguing aspect of constantly challenging young people to assess their misbehaviour is youth work. The constant attrition of getting young people to redress the over or under expression of their powers and remain within normalised boundaries of conduct leaves them demanding to know 'What is it that you want from me?' This is met with our exasperated reply of, 'To grow up!', without either party realising that the constant examination of their appropriateness of young peoples' behaviour is their growing up.

We are not the teacher or the parent who punishes nor the peer group that colludes. Whilst allied to the young person we encourage them to understand their situations from different perspectives, one that challenges them but does not confront. Only within a strong relationship of equality can we help them to reflect on their experience and consider their own participation in the complex and difficult situations they may find themselves in, and how they have a role in restoring conflicts they have constructed. As a result, in treatment programmes for young people that I have designed, we have held a policy of never excluding young people for their behaviour, but instead see these moments of conflict and acting out as opportunities to develop a sense of responsibility to accompany their increasing personal power. Exclusion simply denies the possibility of learning. When we have made this clear to young people they have experienced some fear. But we cannot duck out of life, and if interventions are to be an effective re-creation of preparedness for life, then they cannot be avoided in this arena either. In this way the new demands of the helping relationship of equality not only hold the emerging young person but become a pull on the maturation process itself.

Conclusion

Presently, much is made of measuring outcomes of treatment. Certainly, effective practice is important and young people should be able to access the highest quality services. Yet, there is a shortage of robust research studies which can elucidate what is effective with young people experiencing a range of disorders at present. We must recognise that emerging from their economically and emotionally impoverished lives means that the magnitude of the task of change is often huge for young people with little preparedness for the demands of life. We also know that the effects of interventions tend to be accumulative, with each change attempt setting a higher watermark (Prochaska et al., 1994). For young people, the first attempts at change will be partial in their success but often become interpreted by them as complete failure. But it is what we learn from each change attempt that will prove important in the future, not the failure. As such, the change process can be seen as a failure to process learning rather than a process of failure. Within this jagged recovery, measuring true outcome becomes difficult as setbacks are to be expected and even normalised. Initial reductions in drug use, offending, depression or other behaviours will prove ephemeral but deepen with each change attempt. This leaves us only one true outcome of efficacy. Whether we retain them as they continue to persist through their gains and setbacks. And only the gravity of the human relationship will hold young people in this orbit of change as they spiral towards their goals.

References

Brehm, S.S. and Brehm, J.W. (1981) *Psychological Reactance: A Theory of Freedom and Control.* New York: Academic Press.

Bordin, E. (1979) The Generalizability of the Psychoanalytical Concept of the Working Alliance. *Psychotherapy: Theory, Research and Practice.* 16: 3-Fall.

Dadds, M.R. and McAloon, J. (2002) Prevention. In Essau, C.A. (Ed.) *Substance Abuse and Dependence in Adolescence: Epidemiology, Risk Factors and Treatment.* East Sussex: Brunner-Routledge.

DeShazer, S. cited in Hoyt, M. (Ed.) (1994) *Constructive Therapies.* New York: Guildford Press.

Elliott, J. (2002) Could Do Better? Risk of Cultivating Positive Self-Esteem. *Human Givens: Radical Psychology Today.* 9: 1.

Erikson, E.H. (1994) *Identity: Youth in Crises.* New York: WW Norton and Company.

Erikson, E.H. (1995) *Childhood and Society.* London: Vintage.

Goldman, M.S. et al. (1993) Alcoholism and Memory: Broadening the Scope of Alcohol-expectancy Research. *Psychological Bulletin.* 110.

Kegan, R. (1994) *In Over our Heads: The Mental Demands of Modern Life.* Cambridge, MA: Harvard University Press.

Krupnick, J.L. et al. (1996) The Role of the Therapeutic Alliance in Psychotherapy and Pharmacology Outcome: Findings in the National Institute of Mental Health Treatment of Depression Collaborative Research Program. *Journal of Consulting and Clinical Psychology.* 64: 3.

Lambert, M.J. (1992) Psychotherapy Outcome Research: Implications for Integrative and Eclectic Therapists. In Norcross, J.C. and Goldfried, M.R. (Eds.) *Handbook of Psychotherapy Integration.* New York: Basic Books.

Miller, W.R. and Rollnick, S. (2002) Motivational Interviewing: Preparing People for Change (2nd Edition). New York/London: The Guildford Press.

Patterson, G.R. and Forgatch, M.S. (1985) Therapist Behaviour as a Determinant for Client Noncomplaince: A Paradox for the Behaviour Modifier. *Journal of Consulting and Clinical Psychology.* 53: 6.

Prochaska, J.O. et al. (1994) *Changing for Good.* New York: William Morrow Inc.

Roth, A. and Fonagy, P. (1996) *What Works for Whom? A Critical Review of Psychotherapy Research.* New York: The Guildford Press.

Schwarzer, R. (Ed.) (1992) *Self-Efficacy: Thought Control of Action*. London: Hemisphere Publishing.

Tauber, R.T. (1997) *Self-Fulfilling Prophecy: A Practical Guide to its Use in Education*. Westport: Praegar.

Chapter 9

The Impact of Sibling Substance Misuse on Children and Young People

Nicola Taylor and Jackie Kearney

Introduction

Historically, policy makers, service providers and researchers in the drugs field have approached drug users as individuals rather than as embedded family members. This is slowly beginning to change, with much more recognition and investigation of parental drug use and its impact on other family members, particularly children (Barnard and Barlow, 2003; McKeganey et al., 2003). This largely stems from the fact that the number of women using drugs is on the increase (particularly those of childbearing age) yet service use remains predominantly male (ISDD, 1997; Goode, 2000; Kearney and Taylor, 2001). Recognition of this paradox has led to a number of services conducting research into the impact of family, particularly parental, drug use (Kearney and Taylor, 2001). If government services are to maintain their goal of helping prevent familial dysfunction due to substance misuse by developing and using interventions aimed at substance misusers, they first need to address the fact that many who misuse drugs are part of family systems.

Despite this growing recognition there remains, within the substance abuse literature, limited research in parenting and drug use, and less that addresses the impact of parental drug use on children's lives (Barnard and Barlow, 2003; Cleaver et al., 1999; Elliot et al., 1998; Hogan, 1997, 1999; Klee, Jackson and Lewis, 2002). Many studies have focused on the physiological impact on the pre and post-natal child (Deren, 1986; Ornoy, Michailevskaya, and Lukashov, 1996). The majority of this research has assumed that the mother is the main, or sole, carer (Elliot et al., 1998); and many commentators have tended to discuss parenting and child care as a 'side' issue in relation to service use (Elliot et al., 1998; Hogan, 1997). Within the literature that does address parental drug use there is little focus on fathers as drug using parents (Barnard and Barlow, 2003; Klee, 1998; Ornay, Michailevskaya and Lukashov, 1996) and a general disregard for the family dynamics which are often a serious concern for both the non-drug using family members and the drug using individual (a notable exception is the research by Berridge, 2002).

In terms of sibling drug use this lack of evidence is even more pronounced. The majority of research has been North American in origin, based in the psychological literature and aimed at identifying the propensity of sibling drug use to induce drug use in other family members, particularly other siblings. This research is largely quantitative, and has been driven primarily by a preventative focus (Brook et al., 1983).

A number of recent studies, which tend to be more qualitative in focus, have highlighted the necessity of addressing drug use in a systemic way. That is, by recognising that drug users are part of family and peer systems and are therefore open to familial and peer pressures. And, in turn, that the family and peer groups themselves may also experience consequences of this drug use, only one of which is the increased likelihood of their own drug use beginning or escalating. It is now becoming clear that research into drug use needs to address interpersonal factors such as family systems and processes (e.g. Bachman et al., 1997). One way in which this is being addressed is with the recent proliferation of studies assessing the impact of parental drug use on children and the family system generally (Cleaver et al., 1999).

This chapter is primarily concerned with the impact of sibling substance misuse on both family members and family systems. This will be explored within the context of international findings and current approaches to understanding the aetiology of substance misuse.

We begin by discussing some of the issues and motivations behind involving young people directly in social research. We then go on to outline a local study which investigated broad aspects regarding the impact of drug use on the day-to-day lives of drug using parents and their children. We then discuss current research which has specifically investigated sibling drug use highlighting the similarities between the two groups of findings. We conclude with a discussion of the two clear areas highlighted by previous studies which often influence individuals' propensity to use illicit substances (Brook et al., 1999; Brook et al., 1983).

Throughout 2000 we conducted research with the children of substance using parents. This was part of a larger project which had a number of aims. The overall aim was to access service using and non-service using drug using parents and their children. In itself, this proved a challenge as this is not a particularly easy population to access (e.g. Griffiths, Gossop and Strang, 1993; Renzetti and Lee, 1993; Goode, 2000; Elliott et al., 1998; Taylor and Kearney, 2005). A further aim was to elicit the views of the children of drug using parents about their lifestyles. Given that drug users generally, and drug using parents specifically, are groups which are subject to many stereotypes (Klee, 1998) we wanted to give both the children and the parents an opportunity to speak for themselves about their lives and their drug use. A final aim of the study was an assessment of any additional service needs that our sample felt would be useful. We present a brief discussion of this project and draw out the information on sibling drug use that many of the respondents highlighted. We conclude with a discussion of the key themes raised by both this study and others in relation to sibling drug misuse. Detailed findings of the overall project can be found elsewhere (Kearney and Taylor, 2001; Taylor and Kearney, 2005).

Involving children and young people in sensitive research

The rationale for involving children and young people in research stems from the recognition and understanding that children have their own experience and cultures and therefore rights. During the last ten years, the repositioning of children as independent social actors with their own perspectives has become more prominent in social science research (James and Jenks, 1991; James, Jenks and Prouts, 1999; Mayall, 2003; Waksler, 1991). This view now goes beyond academic theorising, and has become a moral and legal challenge for wider society (Alderson, 1995: 2000; Children's Rights Alliance for England, 2002).

Effective participation in research by children has always been limited (Save the Children, 2001). However, changes in attitude, and legislation, have started to grow from The UN Convention on the Rights of the Child (1989), the Children Act (1989) and tenacious campaigning by numerous children's organisations. Changes in policy over the last decade are also being reflected in the development of major research programmes involving children such as the ESRC Children 5–16 Programme.

Children's increasing participation in research has also resulted in the development of a number of innovative approaches and methods. Some of these have provided a starting point for our methodology (e.g. Beresford 1997; Morrow 1998). Many of these approaches have their roots in phenomenology, ethnography and social anthropology where the methods employed aim to produce intensely qualitative data, eliciting children's reflections on their own lives (e.g. Christensen and James, 2000; Waksler, 1991). There are methodological issues of power and control when doing research with children and young people, as well as complex ethical and legal issues, which can limit and hinder this participatory process. This problem is particularly acute when aiming to include younger children (Alderson, 2000). For further discussion of these issues see Harris, Ch. 8, this volume, and Kearney (Kearney, 2001).

Children living with familial substance abuse – findings

Developing an understanding of the lives of children who live with drug using parents is long overdue (ACMD, 2003; Barnard et al., 2002; Hogan, 1998). There has been relatively little research in the UK about the issue of parental drug misuse. In contrast there has been a proliferation of work around alcohol misuse (Johnson, 1991; Orford and Velleman, 1990). There is even less research that addresses the impact on children (Cleaver et al., 1999; Elliott et al., 1998; Hogan, 1997). Many studies on substance misuse have focussed on the physiological impact (mainly pre-natal and neo-natal) on children (Deren, 1986). A limited number of studies have investigated issues such as the impact on parenting skills, children's needs (usually by proxy) and local service responses to drug using parents (Barnard, 1999; Elliott et al., 1998; Hogan, 1997; McKeganey, Barnard and McIntosh, 2002; Mahoney et al., 2001).

Drawing mostly on literature around alcohol using parents, Cleaver et al.'s report highlights some of the ways that drug and alcohol misuse may have an impact on parenting and children's lives (1999). These include impact on parenting skills, indirect impact on parents with a drug using partner (Greco-Vigorito et al., 1996), distorted parental perceptions (Fergusson et al., 1995), a distorted view of the child (Rutter, 1990), problems with the control of emotions (ChildLine, 1997), the neglect of physical needs, attachment problems (Hogan, 1998; Howe, 1995), behavioural or emotional problems (Owusu-Bempah, 1995; Owusu-Bempah and Howitt, 1997; Rutter, 1990; Amato, 1991) and separation.

Studies of the social and psychological effects on children of parental drug use are similarly relatively scarce (Kumpfer and DeMarsh, 1986) and the findings are mixed. The social consequences highlighted include the impact on living standards, the impact of criminal activities (Hogan, 1998; McKeganey et al., 2002; Swadi, 1994), the loss of friends and family (Leslie, 1993), community rejection (Barnard et al., 2003; Hogan, 1998) and the disruption of family relationships (Barnard et al., 2003; Farmer and Owen, 1995; Vellemen and Orford, 1993).

Research on the cognitive consequences for children seems to be more comprehensive and compelling (Bauman and Levine, 1986). The importance of distinguishing between children exposed pre and post-natal to drugs has been emphasised, as prenatal exposure has been linked to greater problems (Coles, 1992). Such studies are limited in their usefulness as most use retrospective data obtained from pre-selected samples where the parents have, for example, received treatment or been reported for suspected child abuse or neglect. Some of the original US researchers in this field have since modified their conclusions, particularly in relation to so-called crack babies (Goodman, 1992). Researchers now argue that the most damaging consequences for these children actually occurs after they are born, and these are strongly related to continuing conditions of poverty and exclusion (Hurt, 1997). The limitations of previous research also includes the failure to explore the process by which drug use affects parenting, and the meaning it has in children and young peoples' day-to-day lives. Where parenting has been explored, most studies use proxy reporters of the children's experiences (parents, teachers, social workers and so on) rather than talking to the children directly (McKeganey et al., 2002; Hogan, 1996).

More recently, *Hidden Harm*, from the government's Advisory Committee on the Misuse of Drugs (2003) estimates that between 250,000 and 350,000 children live in families where one or both parents are in contact with drug services. High levels of separation are evident, with only 37 per cent of fathers and 64 per cent of mothers living with their children. They identify a range of issues affecting children but acknowledge that many of these are difficult to separate from the common outcomes for children living in 'disadvantaged communities in conditions of poverty and social exclusion' (2003).

A recent large-scale survey of pre-adolescent school children in Scotland identified familial drug use as one of the main sources of exposure to illicit drug use amongst younger children (McIntosh et al., 2003). The issues that most need to be addressed here is the impact of such exposure, and the consequences for children growing up in these circumstances. Orford and Velleman's (1990) work with children whose parents' misused alcohol, identified evidence of resilience that may also occur within other substance misusing families. However, there are also significant differences between alcohol and drug misuse, particularly in relation to criminal subcultures and community responses (Bean, 2002).

Hidden Harm also includes the reporting of an innovative research project with children, where they identify the failure of services to meet the needs of these children in their findings (2003). Again, many of these families experience multiple problems. These children's accounts describe uncertainty and chaos within their daily lives, as well as their exposure to drug use and criminal activities. Children also described their roles as carers and their fear of separation and stigma.

Sibling Substance Misuse

The risks to children of parental substance misuse are becoming better understood (Harbin and Murphy, 2000; Klee et al., 2002; McKeganey et al., 2002). However, the findings from this particular project (Kearney and Taylor, 2001) identified the different risks presented by sibling substance misuse as opposed to parental substance misuse (Windle, 2000). The young people and children interviewed indicated that their parents attempted to avoid exposing their children directly to their drug taking. Any direct exposure was often accidental. This was not necessarily the case where siblings were concerned. There is evidence that the risks are greater between siblings (Brook et al., 2003) particularly in relation to male siblings, and this appears to be supported by these findings. Parents involved in this study repeatedly declared their intention of keeping the worst aspects of misuse from their children (although some did not achieve this). This concern was not always shared by the older siblings of the children involved. It appeared that older siblings openly described the minutiae of their substance use with their younger brothers and sisters and may even have actively shown their siblings how to 'do' it (injecting etc). This has been illustrated in previous studies exploring injecting practices (Stillwell et al., 1999). Figures from this project show that a significant minority of young people had been introduced to substance use by an older sibling, and highlights sibling substance as a potential indicator of risk for children and young people misusing substances themselves in the future.

Sibling drug use is a significantly under-researched area in the UK, with most related findings tied up within research on the impact of peer relationships (Flom et al., 2001) or focussing on smoking and alcohol consumption (Rohde et al., 2003) rather than problematic substance misuse. The literature which does exist identifies a number of key themes which affect the propensity of siblings to experiment with, or regularly use, illicit substances. These themes are in addition to sibling related factors and fit broadly into 'internal' and 'external' influences. Following an overview of the sibling related factors, these themes are discussed below.

External factors

Sibling drug use

Whilst research has consistently shown that sibling modelling of drug use is an important predictive factor (e.g. Brook et al., 1990, 1991) the relationship is not clear cut nor necessarily causal and involves many variables in addition to simple sibling models of drug use. High levels of mutual attachment between siblings has been shown to be a causal factor as has sex of the younger sibling (Brook et al., 1983). Additionally, the impact that sibling factors may or may not have will also depend on the stage of the drug use. In a study of 339 ninth and tenth grade US students Brook et al. (1983) addressed four different stages of drug use:

- non-use
- use of legal drugs
- use of marijuana
- use of illicit drugs other than, or in addition to, marijuana

They discovered that sibling models of drug use were directly linked with the younger sibling's stage of drug use. That is, younger siblings were more likely to abstain from higher end drug use if their siblings did not use drugs. Conversely, exposure to an older brother who did use drugs was likely to 'disinhibit the adolescent's abstention' (Brook et al., 1983: 89). Brook et al. (1999) in an updated study of 278 male college students and their brothers' drug use confirmed that both older brother drug use and a conflict-based relationship between siblings were linked to higher stage drug use.

Peer influences

Studies that have focussed on peer influences have identified clear correlations between peer substance misuse and risk. For example, van den Bree and Pickworth (2005), as part of the National Longitudinal Study of Adolescent Health in the US, assessed the risk factors associated with drug use with 13,718 middle and high school students. They found that peer involvement with substances was one of the strongest predictors of experimental and regular marijuana use. Additionally, the kinds of values peer groups hold, in particular whether they are conventional values or not, has been shown to have an effect on the likelihood of substance experimentation as has parental positive evaluation of peers (Mathias, 1996). Just as peer groups play a part in the unfolding of drug use it appears that adolescent school relationships also play a part. Resnick et al., 1997, found that perceived school connectedness decreased the likelihood of drug use and van den Bree and Pickworth (2005) found that increased levels of school problems often indicated a propensity towards drug use.

Parental factors

Parental drug use has been shown to be a significant factor in the likelihood of children developing substance abuse behaviours as has access to substances within the home (Brook et al., 1999). However, this is further compounded by the levels of attachment between the parent and child (Resnick et al., 1997). Additionally, parental expectations regarding both peer groups and school achievement have been associated with lessening risk taking behaviours (Mathias, 1996; Resnick et al., 1997). In a 1999 study Brook et al. addressed the interplay of family, sibling and peer influences. They discovered that a lack of parent-child attachment and parental drug use were associated with higher end drug use even if the sibling relationship was a positive one. Furthermore, older brother drug use and a conflictual sibling relationship were linked to higher end drug use irrespective of positive parental conditions.

Internal factors

Internal factors which have been shown to affect the chances of adolescents adopting a drug using lifestyle have included levels of rebelliousness and nonconformity (Dobkin et al., 1995) inadequate emotional control and intra-psychic stress (Swaim et al., 1989), self-esteem, involvement in religious and/or pro-social activities and the presence of an adult outside the family that the adolescent is emotionally connected to (Mathias, 1996). However, it appears that the likelihood of siblings to engage in drug using activities is mediated by the interplay of internal, parental, peer and sibling variables.

Limitations and the need for further study

Gender may be an important variable which has traditionally been overlooked in the sparse literature on sibling drug use. One exception to this found that women are more likely to have a sibling or partner and family who are involved in drug use, but the course and severity of their own drug use were less severe (Westermeyer and Boedicker, 2000). However, overall it seems that the aetiology of drug use has significant links with parent/child/sibling attachment relationships and familial drug use. We now turn, finally, to an assessment of differing intervention practices which incorporate an understanding of drug use from an 'individual within the family' perspective.

Interventions

It is imperative that those working with drug users recognise that many of their clients are embedded family members and take account of the potential consequences of this, both to the drug using individual and to the other members of the family. Given that 'a large proportion of young children are exposed to illicit drugs primarily through use of these drugs by family members' (McIntosh et al., 2003: 1615) it may be that this exposure could be targeted as a response to reducing adolescent drug use. Furthermore, family reunification practices may be inappropriate when working with families where drug use remains an issue. We need to review current practice whilst keeping in mind the different roles that various family members may play in mediating, or encouraging, adolescent drug use (Maluccio and Ainsworth, 2003).

Conclusion

Sibling drug use may play a part in encouraging adolescent drug use, but just as importantly positive sibling relationships may also play a part in preventing drug use, or at least in preventing its progression. This may be an important way for various drug use services to access and better serve their clients. Above all, it is imperative that policy makers, service providers and researchers alike recognise that drug users are often part of a wider family unit and that this family unit will impact upon their drug use in some way, whether positively or negatively.

References

Alderson, P. (1995) *Listening to Children: Children, Ethics and Social Research*. Barkingside: Barnardo's.

Alderson, P. (2000) *Young Children's Rights: Exploring Beliefs, Principles and Practice*. London: Jessica Kingsley.

Amato, P. (1991) Parental Absence During Childhood and Depression in Later Life. *Sociological Quarterly*. 32: 4, 543–46.

Bachman, J. et al. (1997) *Smoking, Drinking and Drug Use in Young Adulthood: The Impacts of New Freedoms and New Responsibilities*. Hillsdale, NJ: Erlbaum.

Barnard, M. (1999) Forbidden Questions: Drug-dependent Parents and the Welfare of their Children: Editorial. *Addiction*. 94: 8, 1109–11.

Barnard, M. and Barlow, J. (2003) Discovering Parental Drug Dependence: Silence and Disclosure. *Children and Society*. 17, 45–56.

Bauman, P.S. and Levine, S.A. (1986) The Development of Children of Drug Addicts. *International Journal of Addiction*. 21, 849–63.

Bean, P. (2002) *Drugs and Crime*. Devon: Willan Publishing.

Beresford, B. (1997) *Personal Accounts Involving Disabled Children in Research*. London: HMSO.

Berridge, V. (2002) Substance Abuse and the Compromise of Fathering. *Addiction*. 97: 1117.

Brook, J., Brook, D. and Whiteman, M. (1999) Older Sibling Correlates of Younger Sibling Drug Use in the Context of Parent-child Relations. *Genetic, Social, and General Psychology Monographs*. 125: 4, 451.

Brook, J. et al. (1983) Older Brother's Influence on Younger Sibling's Drug Use. *The Journal of Psychology*. 114: 83–90.

Children's Rights Alliance for England (2002) *State of Children's Rights in England: A Report on the Implementation of the Convention on the Rights of the Child*. www.crights.org.uk/pdfs/StateofChildrensRights.pdf

Christensen, P. and James, A. (Eds.) (2000) *Research with Children – Perspectives and Practices*. London: Falmer Press.

Cleaver, H., Unell, I. and Aldgate, J. (1999) *Children's Needs: Parenting Capacity. The Impact of Parental Mental Illness, Problem Alcohol and Drug Use, and Domestic Violence on Children's Development*. London: The Stationery Office.

Coles, C.D. (1992) Effects of Cocaine and Alcohol Use in Pregnancy on Neonatal Growth and Neurobehavioral Status. *Neurotoxicology and Teratology*. 14: 23–33.

Deren, S. (1986) Children of Substance Abusers: A Review of the Literature. *Journal of Substance Abuse Treatment*. 3: 77–94.

Dobkin, P. et al. (1995) Individual and Peer Characteristics in Predicting Boys' Early Onset of Substance Abuse: A Seven-year Longitudinal Study. *Child Development*. 66: 1198–214.

Elliott, E. et al. (1998) *Fit to be a Parent: The Needs of Drug Using Parents in Salford and Trafford*. Salford: PHRRC Research Report No. 8.

Farmer, E. and Owen, M. (1995) *Child Protection Practice: Private Risks and Public Remedies*. London: HMSO.

Fergusson, D.M., Horwood, I.J. and Lynskey, M.T. (1995) Maternal Depressive Symptoms and Depressive Symptoms in Adolescence. *Journal of Psychology and Psychiatry*. 36: 7, 1161–78.

Flom, P. et al. (2001) Recalled Adolescent Peer Norms towards Drug Use in Young Adulthood in a Low Income, Minority Urban Neighbourhood. *Journal of Drug Issues*. 31: 2, 425–43.

Goode, S. (2000) Researching a Hard-to-Access and Vulnerable Population: Some Considerations on Researching Drug and Alcohol-Using Mothers. *Sociological Research Online*, 5:1. http://www.socresonline.org.uk/5/1/goode.html

Goodman, E. (1992) The Myth of the Crack Babies. *The Boston Sunday Globe*. January 12th 69, http://www.druglibrary.org/schaffer/cocaine/crackbb2.htm.

Greco-Vigorito, C. et al. (1996) Affective Symptoms in Young Children of Substance Abusers Correlate with Parental Distress. *Psychological Reports*. 79: 2, 547–52.

Griffiths, P., Gossop, M. and Strang, J. (1993) Reaching Hidden Populations of Drug Users by Privileged Access Interviewers: Methodological and Practical Issues. *Addiction*. 88: 1617–26.

Harbin, F, and Murphy, M. (2000) *Substance Misuse and Childcare: How to Understand, Assist and Intervene when Drugs Affect Parenting*. Lyme Regis: Russell House Publishing.

Hogan, D. (1997) *The Social and Psychological Needs of Children of Drug Users: Report on an Exploratory Study*. Dublin: The Children's Research Centre, Trinity College.

Hogan, D. (1999) The Psychological Development and Welfare of Children of Opiate and Cocaine Users: Review and Research Needs. *Journal of Child Psychology and Psychiatry.* 39: 5, 609–20.

Howe, D. (1995) *Attachment Theory for Social Work Practice.* London: Macmillan.

Hurt, H. (1997) A Prospective Evaluation of Early Language Development in Children with In-utero Cocaine Exposure and in Control Subjects. *Journal of Paediatrics.* 130, 310–2.

ISDD (1996) *UK National Report for the European Monitoring Centre for Drugs and Drug Addiction.* London: Institute for the Study of Drug Dependence.

James, A. and Jenks, C. (Eds.) (1991) *Constructing and Reconstructing Childhood.* London: Polity Press.

James, A., Jenks, C. and Prout, A. (1999) *Theorizing Childhood.* London: Polity Press.

Johnson, J. (1991) Forgotten no Longer: An Overview of Research on Children of Chemically Dependent Parents. In Rivinus, T.M. (Ed.) *Children of Chemically Dependent Parents.* New York: Brunner Publishers.

Kearney, J. and Taylor, N. (2001) *The Highs and Lows of Family Life.* IPHRP Research Report, University of Salford.

Kearney, J., Harbin, F., Murphy, M., Wheeler, E. and Whittle, J. (2005) *The Highs and Lows of Family Life: Familial Substance Misuse from a Child's Perspective.* Bolton: Bolton ACPC Research Report.

Klee, H. (1998) Drug-using Parents: Analysing the Stereotypes. *International Journal of Drug Policy.* 9: 437–48.

Klee, H., Jackson, M. and Lewis, S. (2002) *Drug Misuse and Motherhood.* London: Routledge.

Kumpfer, K.L. and DeMarsh, J. (1986) Family-oriented Interventions for the Prevention of Chemical Dependency in Children and Adolescents. In Griswold-Ezekoye, S., Kumpfer, K.L. and Bukoski, W.J. (Eds.) *Childhood and Chemical Abuse: Prevention and Intervention.* New York: Hayworth Press.

Leslie, B. (1993) Casework and Client Characteristics of Cocaine Crack Using Parents in a Child Welfare Setting. *The Journal of the Ontario Association of Children's Aid Societies.*

Mahoney, C. and MacKechnie, N. (2001) *In a Different World.* Liverpool DAAT and Barnardos.

Maluccio, A. and Ainsworth, F. (2003) Drug Use by Parents: A Challenge for Family Reunification Practice. *Children and Youth Services Review.* 25: 7, 511–33.

Mayall, B. (2003) *Children's Childhoods Observed and Experienced.* London: Falmer Press.

Mathias, R. (1996) *Protective Factors can Buffer High-risk Youths from Drug Use.* NIDA Notes, 11: 3.

McIntosh, J. et al. (2003) Exposure to Drugs among Pre-teenage School Children. *Addiction.* 98: 11, 1615–23.

McKeganey, N., Barnard, M. and McIntosh, J. (2002) Paying the Price for their Parents' Addiction: Meeting the Needs of the Children of Drug-using Parents. *Drugs: Education, Prevention and Policy.* 9: 233–46.

McKeganey, N., McIntosh, J. and MacDonald, F. (2003) Young People's Experience of Illegal Drug Use in the Family. *Drugs: Education, Prevention and Policy.* 10: 2, 169–84.

McMahon, T. and Rounsaville, B. (2002a) Substance Abuse and Fathering: Adding Poppa to the Research Agenda. *Addiction.* 97: 1109–15.

McMahon, T. and Rounsaville, B. (2002b) Substance Abuse and Fathering: Some Final Comments on Context and Process. *Addiction.* 97: 1120–2.

Morrow, V. (1998) *Understanding Families: Children's Perspectives.* London: NCB.

Orford, J. and Velleman, R. (1990) Offspring of Parents with Drinking Problems: Drinking and Drug Taking as Young Adults. *British Journal of Addiction.* 85: 770–94.

Ornoy, A., Michailevskaya, V. and Lukashov, I. (1996) The Developmental Outcome of Children Born to Heroin-dependant Mothers, Raised at Home or Adopted. *Child Abuse and Neglect.* 20: 5, 385–96.

Owusu-Bempah, J. (1995) Information about the Absent Parent as a Factor in the Well-being of Children of Single-parent Families. *International Social Work.* 38: 253–75.

Owusu-Bempah, J. and Howitt, J. (1997) *Self-identity and Black Children in Care.* cited in Cleaver et al., (1999), op. cit.

Parke, R. (2002) Substance Abusing Fathers: Descriptive, Process and Methodological Perspectives. *Addiction.* 97, 1117–8.

Phares, V. (2002) Finding Poppa in Substance Abuse Research. *Addiction.* 97, 1119–20.

Renzetti, C. and Lee, R. (Eds.) (1993) *Researching Sensitive Topics.* Newbury Park: Sage.

Resnick, M. et al. (1997) Protecting Adolescents from Harm. Findings from the National Longitudinal Study on Adolescent Health. *Journal of the American Medical Association.* 278: 10, 823–32.

Rutter, M. (1990) Commentary: Some Focus and Process Considerations Regarding Effects of Parental Depression on Children. *Developmental Psychology.* 26, 60–7.

Rohde, P. et al. (2003) Psychiatric Disorders, Familial Factors and Cigarette Smoking: Associations with Smoking Initiations. *Nicotine and Tobacco Research.* 5: 1, 85–98.

Save the Children (2001) *Children's Rights: A Second Chance.* Plymouth: International Children Rights Alliance.

Smart, C. and Neale, B. (1997) Experiments with Parenthood. *Sociology.* 31: 2, 201–19.

Smith, D. (1987) *The Everyday World as Problematic.* Boston: North-eastern University Press.

Stillwell, G. et al. (1999) The Modelling of Injecting Behaviour and Initiation into Injecting. *Addiction Research.* 7: 5, 447–59.

Swadi, H. (1994) Parenting Capacity and Substance Misuse: An Assessment Scheme. *ACPP Review and Newsletter.* 16: 5, 237–44.

Swaim, E. et al. (1989) Links from Emotional Distress to Adolescent Drug Use: A Path Model. *Journal of Consulting and Clinical Psychology.* 57, 227–31.

Taylor, N. and Kearney, J. (2005) Researching Hard-to Reach Populations: Privileged Access, Interviewers and Drug Using Parents. *Sociological Research Online.* 10: 2.

Van den Bree, M. and Pickworth, W. (2005) Risk Factors: Predicting Changes in Marijuana Involvement in Teenagers. *Archives of General Psychiatry.* 62, 311–9.

Velleman, R. (1993) Alcohol and Drug Problems in Parents: An Overview of the Impact on Children and the Implications for Practice. In Gopfert, M., Webster, J. and Seeman, M. (Eds.) *Parental Psychiatric Disorder: Distressed Parents and Their Families.* Cambridge University Press.

Waksler, F. (1991) *Studying the Social Worlds of Children: Sociological Readings.* London: Falmer Press.

Westermeyer, J. and Boedicker, E. (2000) Course, Severity, and Treatment of Substance Abuse Among Women Versus Men. *The American Journal of Drug and Alcohol Abuse.* 26: 4, 523–35.

Windle, M. (2000) Parental, Sibling and Peer Influence on Adolescent Substance Use and Alcohol Problems. *Applied Developmental Science.* 4: 2, 98–110.

Chapter 10

Setting up a Substance Misuse Project for Young People

Tom O'Loughlin and Dave Seaber

Introduction

This chapter outlines the experience of setting up a substance misuse project for children and young people and their families in Bolton. In 1998, there had been increasing concern in the area about the number of young people who were seeking assistance from the adult community drug team. Also, there was increasing awareness within young people's services of the problems of substance misuse and substance dependency. In particular, there was an awareness of the use of heroin by a significant number of young people. Over a third of users reporting to the adult services had started using opiates before they were nineteen.

In October 1998, Bolton Social Services Department created a new post of a social worker to work directly with young people misusing substances. Initially the worker operated from a youth service resource centre. By January 1999 a caseload of 32 young people had been accumulated. Ages ranged from 10 to 15 years old, with the greatest concentration at the top end of this age scale. Opiates were the most common drug used. The social worker expressed concern at the easy access to a range of substances and the number of young people injecting heroin.

All this information was shared with the drug action team and its co-ordinator. There was close collaboration with the primary care trust who subsequently seconded two full-time workers who joined the social worker in undertaking the direct work with young people. One of these workers was a nurse, the second was a youth worker with experience of adult substance treatment. There was also agreement to allocate sessional time from the substance misuse specialist doctor to work with these young people.

What informed the early development of a separate service?

We were influenced by a number of significant policy documents available at this time. These included *To Build a Better Britain*, the 10-year National Drug Strategy 1997,

Drug Related Early Intervention, Developing Services for Young People and Families, SCODA 1997, *Children and Young People, Guidance for Commissioners and Providers of Substance Misuse Services*, London Drug Policy Forum 1997 and *Children and Young People Substance Misuse Services*, NHS Health Advisory Service Report 1998. All these documents identified similar principles and themes. The major one was the importance of services for children, young people and families being provided separately to adult services.

In particular, a document produced jointly by SCODA and the Children's Legal Centre, *Young People and Drugs, Policy Guidance for Drugs Interventions* (1999) established 10 key principles to be applied in developing policy and practice. These are:

- A child or young person is not an adult.
- The overall welfare of the individual child or young person is of paramount importance.
- The views of the young person are of central importance and should always be sought and considered.
- Services need to respect parental responsibility when working with a young person.
- Services should recognise and co-operate with the local authority in carrying out its responsibility towards young people.
- A holistic approach is vital at all levels, as young people's needs do not respect professional boundaries.
- Services must be child-centred.
- A comprehensive range of services needs to be provided.
- Services must be competent.
- Services should aim to operate in all cases according to the principles of good practice.

This document was of particular significance. The service was built around existing guidance and research and the perceived needs of young people in our area.

As part of its early work, the project worked hard to establish our mission statement. This is to:

Identify and intervene early with young people and their families regarding their substance misuse related problems, focusing particularly on high risk groups. To offer a range of education, prevention treatment and rehabilitation aimed at minimising risk and maximising health, social and psychological wellbeing.

An external needs assessment and evaluation was provided by a researcher from Manchester University (Kenny, 2001). This significantly helped the project's development. The report concluded, 'the need for a discrete substance misuse service for young people is clearly evident and it is anticipated that referrals will continue to increase'. Also, that 'the service is well placed to develop services at Tiers 2, 3 and 4 and its role in the wider young person's substance misuse strategy is central'.

The report identified a number of pointers for future developments. These have been followed through and provided a helpful checklist for the project's development.

As the team became established, there was a desire to find an appropriate name for the service and eventually 'Project 360°' was agreed, inspired by the need to meet need from all angles and the desire to turn young people's lives around.

We believe that one of the strengths of the service is that it stands apart from (or between) other main service providers to young people. This meant that Project 360° could develop an integrated health, social care and youth service provision from one location and one multi-disciplinary team. This means that children, young people and families do not have to be passed around from one service to another, but that they could be offered a full range of interventions from one service, or a one-stop shop.

In 2001, funding was made available to the Youth Offending Team (YOT) for substance misuse work. Rather than set up specialist workers within the YOT, it was agreed to use this funding to create two further posts in the young people's team, a substance misuse worker and a family support worker. A protocol was agreed for the YOT to receive services for young offenders with substance misuse problems and training and consultation. In this way, any young offenders can benefit from the combined resources of the multi-disciplinary team and substance misuse services were not seen as solely part of a crime reduction intervention.

The importance and the development of the interagency team

Agencies in Bolton were committed to work to these principles. There was also a strong commitment to target the most vulnerable young people; those who had developed dependency and needed intensive support and help. We were not working with a population that rationally chose recreational substance use as one part of an 'average' lifestyle (Parker et al., 1998). What we had discovered was that we were working with a discrete sub-set of socially excluded young people with multiple vulnerabilities, for whom substance was either only part of the problem, or actively used to ease the distress of their situation: 'In a confusing, frightening and ever-changing world heroin acts as the ultimate safety net. For the price of a bag, heroin will take you to a safe, warm place every time' (Gilman, 2000: 24).

The need for a holistic service supported the development of a multi-disciplinary team. As Gilman (2000: 22) reminds us:

> *Social exclusion comes about as a result of a whole range of factors compounding each other. Social exclusion represents a package of 'joined up' problems. Heavy end substance misuse is woven into social exclusion and therefore requires a genuinely 'joined up' solution.*

There had been a good basis for achieving this with the designated posts agreed by the social services department and the primary care trust. The social worker and the two staff seconded from the Primary Care Trust came from different backgrounds and brought different practice experience.

This was followed by the provision of sessional support from a substance misuse specialist that meant that clinical interventions could be offered where appropriate to young people. This was followed up by agreement for sessional support from a community paediatrician and a consultant from CAMHS. This meant that all significant areas of children and young people's medical needs could be addressed.

Following discussion and collaboration between the youth offending team manager, the drug action team co-ordinator and managers in the social services department and the primary care trust, a grant was secured from the Youth Justice Board to further develop the service. This included the renting of office space for the staff in a young person's centre. This centre was specifically chosen as it housed a number of different services for young people, thereby avoiding stigma and providing a base for a one-stop shop service.

The grant allowed the creation of additional posts, a family support worker to work with parents and carers of the young people, a team leader to provide management and leadership for the team and a full-time administrator. When the Youth Justice Board funding ended, the Drug Action Team Joint Commissioning Group took on responsibility for funding services so that the project could consolidate and continue, but also expand into new areas of need.

A detailed policy and procedural document was prepared which covered issues of health and safety, consent and confidentiality, parental involvement, children and young people's rights. This document was agreed by the drug action team, the area child protection committee and the joint strategy team for children.

Developing common skills

Initially we needed to identify what assessment and intervention work could be undertaken with these young people. There was a desire to establish a core key worker function that could be undertaken by workers from different backgrounds, to avoid young people having to be passed around different members of the team. The early coming together of practitioners from different backgrounds generated not just a sense of team, but a shared core of knowledge and skills. Therefore, a general substance misuse role was developed and agreed with the workers. This included providing the support to young people on substance misuse prescribing programmes. Eventually, an agreed substance misuse worker job description and person specification was identified.

The strategy that developed therefore was that workers from different backgrounds shared a common role in their key worker duties to young people, but retained their specialist knowledge and skills which they shared within the team by providing consultation to colleagues. A balance was therefore achieved between protecting and ensuring the personal development of workers with different qualifications and backgrounds, and developing a core substance misuse key worker role that could be provided by all the young people's workers in the team. Naturally the nurse has particular additional functions that cannot be undertaken by other members of the team in relation to health interventions, but apart from these, young people have the benefit of one key worker supporting their care plan.

In March 2001, the drug action team commissioned a post of Young Person's Substance Misuse Training Co-ordinator. This post has responsibility for training needs analysis, the organisation, co-ordination and presentation of training on substance misuse and the development of a multi-disciplinary training pool to assist in the delivery of this service. A close relationship between this post-holder and the staff of the young people's team was established to help deliver the multi-agency training programme. Members of the team would both benefit from the training provision and would offer their skills in developing the training for staff from other services.

Making the service accessible

Misusing substances impacts massively on the health and well being of children and young people. It is widely recognised that adolescents in particular do not readily access formal health and social care services. Waiting lists, age limits, inflexible appointment times and restricted hours of working all reduce the chances of young people engaging with services. The young people who lead chaotic lives due to their substance misuse are even less likely to attend mainstream services They require a much more creative, flexible and informal approach. The ethos of Project 360° suggested the provision of a service that encouraged self-referral and was accessible; that was flexible, non-stigmatising and included work out of hours; that offered a choice between centre-based work or community and home-based visits and that had age appropriate interventions and that was solution focused. This way of working is central to how services are provided at Project 360°.

The strengths of the developing service were considerable and the staff involved were enthusiastic and excited by the opportunities available. The service established and maintained a very strong children and young people centred approach. The availability of the family support workers also ensured that all parents and carers of children/young people referred could be offered separate support. Initially outreach work undertaken by the team included attendance at community venues, the communication and dissemination of information with other children and youth services. There are plans to develop an assertive outreach service.

The involvement of children, young people and families in the service has been maintained through a requirement that there is full involvement in all assessments and interventions. Feedback has been secured through the use of questionnaires, which are subsequently collated and included as part of the service's performance review. These show significant satisfaction with the service and staff and, in particular, a stated willingness to return to the service if problems reoccur.

The wider health and social care agenda

All children, young people and families referred are offered advice, information and consultation as appropriate. Assessments are undertaken and consist of a brief assessment completed within seven working days and fuller, more complex assessments as necessary within 35 working days. Social care services available from Project 360° include counselling, motivational interviewing, brief therapy and crisis intervention.

The effective use of diversionary activities from the range of preventative services available from young people's services is also encouraged by the team. This is essential in trying to help young people develop a more positive lifestyle and optimistic outlook. Provision of support from the family support workers includes the availability of group work with parents, siblings and children of substance misusers.

The team has a significant health care role. In addition to a social care assessment, all young people engaged with Project 360° have access to a health assessment. These assessments provide the opportunity to consider the physical, sexual and psychological well being of the child or young person and plan the most appropriate intervention.

The health care part of the team includes a paediatric nurse, a specialist who is family planning trained and a nurse prescriber, a community paediatrician, a consultant in substance misuse with support from a consultant in CAMHS. Catch-up immunisation programmes are offered to all young people who require them. Also, dental, visual and dietary advice is included. As both the nurse and the paediatrician are able to prescribe, treatment can be provided for a variety of ailments associated with substance misuse, for example chest infections, abscesses, cellulitis.

As substance misuse and risky sexual behaviour in young people have an association, the nurse and paediatrician both provide comprehensive contraception and sexual health advice to the young people and are able to prescribe contraceptives if appropriate. Project 360° receives funding from teenage pregnancy monies to offer testing for chlamydia to both young men and women. A sexual health worker has recently joined the team.

As young people who misuse substances are at risk from blood borne viruses, especially those involved in injecting, all young people are offered Hepatitis B immunisation and injecting users are also offered Hepatitis A immunisation.

A needle exchange service is offered on a named young person basis, in accordance with the safeguards and procedures in the team's policy and procedural document. Team members have skills in the use of electro-stimulation therapy, which can be effective in helping young people come off substances. Sessional support from the specialist doctor in substance misuse enables young people to access a range of substitute prescribing interventions and, as part of this, they are supported on an intensive basis by the substance misuse workers. There is also provision to undertake community detoxification when necessary.

The team developed very close links with a new in-patient detoxification unit for young people at Kenyon House, which opened at Prestwich Hospital in 2002. In 2002–3 six young people from Bolton were referred to this unit by the staff at Project 360° and supported throughout their stay and on discharge.

Also, as and when necessary, young people can be referred to residential rehabilitation placements following detoxification and three young people have been referred for this service since Project 360°'s creation.

Demand and performance indicators

The demand for the service increased from the start. From 1 April 1999 to 31 March 2000, the project received 44 referrals, 20 of which were related to heroin use. From 1 April 2000 to 31 March 2001, 160 referrals were received. The main substances identified were cannabis, 31 per cent, heroin 24 per cent and alcohol 19 per cent. From 1 April 2002 to 31 March 2003, 191 referrals were received. Again alcohol, cannabis and heroin were the main reasons for referral.

The service decided to measure its work against the National Quality Protects Standards for children and for the year 2002–3, 83.3 per cent of initial assessments were completed within seven working days and 96.8 per cent more complex assessments were completed within 35 working days. There was only one repeat referral of the same need recorded.

To ensure that the service was in line with the recommendations of the Laming Inquiry, case file audits have been completed on a three-monthly basis. These audits have identified that improvements need to be made in the recording of young people's wishes and feelings, care plans need to be sharper, include timescales and that a six-month minimum review process needs to be implemented. Plans to achieve these changes have been put in place.

In 2002–3 the average waiting time to see a member of the project team was just over three days, with the longest waiting period two weeks for an appointment. Priorities were given for appointments to the young people with the most urgent need, who were usually seen on the same day. Project 360° has a good record since its inception in engaging with service users. The fallout rate, either through failing to take up offers of a service or ending the service prior to an agreed closure, has averaged at 30 per cent of all referrals. Many of the young people who failed to engage were from referrals from other professionals rather than the actual young person and often in relation to low level cannabis use when the young person was reluctant to engage.

The project has a good record for engaging young people with opiate dependency and injecting behaviour. For this client group, considerable efforts are made by the team to maintain contact and overcome initial resistance.

Impact on other systems/practitioners

It is impossible for Project 360° to work with all children and young people with a substance issue in our area. Although the project developed to work at Tiers 3 to 4, these young people still need services from other practitioners. There are also a significant number of young people at the Tier 2 stage that need services from all the practitioners around them. One of the team's most crucial roles is to attempt to help make other practitioners more comfortable working with substance misuse and multiple problem vulnerable young people. Although the transfer of knowledge and confidence from a central team is not a straightforward affair (Murphy, 1996) the team is attempting to offer a consultation service for all practitioners struggling with young peoples' substance abuse.

Problems and implications

As the multi-disciplinary team was a new development and also innovative, there was a need to develop practices in all areas. Referral and assessment forms were developed specifically to be child, young person and family centred and based on the *National Assessment Framework for Children in Need.* They also interlinked with Bolton's Child Concern Model and multi-disciplinary team approach to work with children in need (Jones and O'Loughlin, 2003). Case files were developed on a modular basis to include the health related work and, when appropriate, details of clinical interventions.

There was a necessity to try to develop a database to record information about activity and performance. Issues in relation to IT and the accessibility of information from different agencies also required attention. For example, it took some time to try to get agreement from staff from the primary care trust to be able to directly access electronically information about children and families in social services. This is not to say that the problems about developing appropriate systems for administration and addressing the thorny issue of recording and confidentiality have been completely overcome. We, like most other integrated interagency teams, are striving to reach workable compromises between the needs of the young person, their parents and all the practice groups involved in their care. What we do know is that adult models of administration and recording do not fit the needs of these young people.

Conclusion

We know that the setting up of our service was in response to a particular set of local circumstances (Murphy and Harbin, 2000) but we would like to offer some messages that will be more universally applicable.

There is a real need to be flexible whilst developing your services so that what is finally achieved 'fits' the needs of young people, families and agencies in your area.

Whatever services are developed, it is crucial that it breaks down the traditional barriers between adult and children's services on the one hand (Kearney et al., 2000) and substance and child care services on the other (Murphy and Oulds, 2000). These traditional barriers to collaboration are neither understood nor approved of by our young users. For them the one-stop shop and single key worker system make good sense.

It is very important to be owned by all key stakeholders, including the young people, and this really assists in the development of interagency collaboration and resources. It is also important to be successful in attracting resources from many different sources, both to maintain what has been established and to evaluate and develop what needs to be improved.

Finally, and most importantly, it is crucial to be accessible to the children and young people whose needs you are trying to meet. This is not a group of service users who arrive and stay easily. Anything that you can do to attract and then keep them, will radically improve the effectiveness of your service.

References

Gilman, M. (2000) Social Exclusion and Drug Using Parents. In Harbin, F. and Murphy, M. *Substance Misuse and Childcare.* Lyme Regis: Russell House Publishing.

Home Office (1997) *To Build a Better Britain.* London: HMSO.

Jones, L. and O'Loughlin, T. (2003) A Child Concern Model to Embrace the Framework. In Calder, M. and Hackett, S. *Assessment in Child Care.* Lyme Regis: Russell House Publishing.

Kearney, P., Levin, E. and Rosen, G. (2000) *Alcohol, Drug and Mental Health Problems: Working with Families.* London: NISW.

Kenny, S. (2001*) An Evaluation of Bolton's Young People's Substance Misuse Service.* Bolton DAT.

London Drug Policy Forum (1997) *Children and Young People: Guidance for Commissioners and Providers of Substance Misuse Services.* London: LDPF.

Murphy, M. (1996) *The Child Protection Unit: Its History, Function and Effectiveness in the Organisation of Child Protection Work.* Aldershot: Ashgate.

Murphy, M. and Harbin, F. (2000) Background and Current Context of Substance Misuse and Childcare. In Harbin, F. and Murphy, M. *Substance Misuse and Childcare.* Lyme Regis: Russell House Publishing.

Murphy, M. and Oulds, G. (2000) Establishing and Developing Co-operative Links. In Harbin, F. and Murphy, M. *Substance Misuse and Childcare.* Lyme Regis: Russell House Publishing.

NHS Health Advisory Service (1998) *Children and Young People Substance Misuse Services.* London: DOH.

Parker, H., Aldridge, J. and Measham, F. (1998) *Illegal Leisure: The Normalisation of Adolescent Recreational Drug Use.* London: Routledge.

SCODA (1997) *Drug Related Early Intervention: Devloping Services for Young People and Families.* London: Local Government Drug Forum.

SCODA/Children's Legal Centre (1999) *Young People and Drugs, Policy Guidance for Drugs Interventions.* London: LGDF.